Beginner's to the Stock Market

The easiest proven strategies, the right trading psychology, the big mistakes to avoid.
All you need to know to make money in stocks today and grow your wealth

Martin Wilder

Table of Contents

By the same author:

This is a perfect guide if you are looking for a new way to build your financial freedom, working from home or wherever you want. All the secrets to creating a profitable business online, and all the tips to avoid mistakes that will make you waste time and money

Introduction

Congratulations on purchasing *Beginner's Guide to the Stock Market*, and thank you for doing so.

The following chapters will discuss the various topics that those beginning in the stock investing world should familiarize themselves with. Chapter 1 will discuss the basics of the stock market. This includes basic terminology that beginners should familiarize themselves with, the concept of risk, different methods of investing (DIY, Robo-advisors, and financial advisors), the concept of leverage, basics about the global economic market, and how it operates, and economic crashes vs. economic corrections. The second chapter will focus on the pros and cons of investing in stocks and compare an investment to other common investments. The pros and cons of putting one's money in stocks, bank accounts, real estate, bonds, and physical objects will be discussed. Chapter 3 will discuss how to set proper goals for investing. These goals include how much to invest, how much risk the investor should be willing to take, how much growth should be desired, how much portfolio diversification the investor should strive for, and how to decide whether the individual should save, invest, or pay off their debt first. The fourth chapter describes how to start. The investor will need to choose an investing method, choose a stockbroker, open an account, make an initial investment and link an account, and start trading stocks. These actions are detailed further in this chapter. Chapter 5 will further explain the various investing possibilities that are open to investors. These include the options to trade in the short-term or buy and hold for the long-term, use stock options, trade forex stocks, trade common or preferred stocks, have different order types on stocks, and invest in a variety of funds. The sixth chapter discusses how to find the proper stock or stocks to invest in at first. This includes deciding whether to invest in one stock or several, how to come up with familiar companies to invest in, how to discover "new" companies to invest in, how to find the proper investment for the desired time period, how many prices and shares to start off buying, and how to analyze stock charts to determine if the company will prove to be a wise investment. Chapter 7 will explain several trading strategies for the trader to practice, how to determine when to buy and hold vs. when to trade, bull vs. bear, how to buy low and sell high, and what to do in a negative market trend. Chapter 8 discusses several errors to avoid, such as common beginners' mistakes, diversification issues, and problems with speculation. Chapter 9 will teach investors how to establish the proper trading mindset, practice self-discipline, and practice good trading methods. Chapter 10 discusses additional tips and tricks for the trader to use, such as how to maximize one's investments, how to use 401k, 403b, and IRA to one's advantage, direct stock purchase plans, and dividend reinvestment plans.

There are plenty of books on this subject on the market, so thanks again for choosing this one! Every effort was made to ensure it is full of as much useful information as possible. Please enjoy it!

Chapter 1: Stock Market Basics

When starting out in the stock investment world, there will be a lot of unfamiliar terms and procedures that you must become familiar with to be successful in investing. Many individuals fail to begin to invest in stock because it is so different from the typical banking experience. Although it will take time to educate yourself on the stock market, that time will definitely be beneficial to you. Once you learn more about the stock market, you will possess a greater understanding of the global economic market. This further understanding will allow you to multiply your money and generate passive income.

Stock: Common Terms and What it is

The stock market is a whole other world. What is stock, and why do companies allow consumers to purchase it? What is volatility? Some terms and processes seem completely foreign to those who aren't involved in stock. Familiarizing yourself with even the basics of stock can prove highly beneficial to your ability to buy, sell, and trade stock effectively. It is important to understand what stock is. It's common knowledge that stock is a way to invest one's money. What exactly is it, though? Stock is essentially buying a very small share of a company. This allows companies to receive money from investors. In return, the investors own a portion of the company. This means that the investors are subject to the same rises and falls of the company as a whole. The stock is sold from the company to a stock market exchange (through the initial public offering process), then to stockbrokers, then to the investors.

The stock market is incredibly large; there are many stocks out there. To make it easier to track, there are a few major stock market indexes. The three major indexes in the United States are the S&P 500, Dow Jones Industrial Average, and Nasdaq Composite. These indexes are major indicators of how the stock market is performing. Indexes are primarily created based upon the categorization of stock into different capitalization and sector segregation groups. The "stock market" is often referring to one or more indexes, as they are great indicators of the stock market's performance.

The stock market is much like an auction. Buyers will bid for the stock, which means that they are telling the sellers what the highest price they are willing to pay for the stock is. In return, the sellers will ask for a certain price. The gap between these two prices is known as the bid-ask spread, which must be closed for a successful trade. There are a number of terms that you must familiarize yourself with to understand the stock market better. These are crucial for maximizing your trading potential.

- **Beta**: The beta measures how price and movement are related. The beta is calculated by the amount of points that a stock will move for every point of movement in the market.

- **Capitalization**: This is the supposed market value of a company's stock.

- **Dividends**: Although many investors trade with the hope of an increase in the stock's value, dividends are an added bonus for many stocks. Dividends are essentially a company's "gift" to you for investing with them. This is when a small portion of their earnings is paid to the shareholders. Dividends are commonly paid out either quarterly or annually.

- **Highs and Lows**: These are achieved when the stock or index reaches a greater or lower point than it did previously for its price.

- **Liquidity**: This is the level of ease of getting in and out of stock.

- **Margin**: When the investor borrows the broker's money for the purchase of stock, the difference between the loan amount and price is known as the margin.

- **Open and Close**: The United States stock market opens at 9:30 a.m. EST and closes at 4:00 p.m.

- **Passive Income**: When you invest, you will be generating passive income. This means that instead of working for a dollar amount for each hour you work, you will (quite literally) make money while you sleep.

- **Portfolio**: An investor's portfolio is the collection of all of the investments that they own.

- **Short-Selling**: This is when the investor borrows shares from another with the intention to return it later. The intention is to sell the shares at a higher price now, then buy them back once the price decreases later. This is a wise move for stock that seems to have a decrease in the near future.

- **Stock Symbol**: This is a way of identifying stock. Symbols are alphabetic and are one to four letters long.

- **Volatility**: This describes the overall price movements of the market. If a stock is highly volatile, it changes greatly every day.

- **Volume**: This is how much stock is traded in a time period, whether it is for the whole market or one particular investor.

- **Yield**: This is how much you are making on the investment. A high yield means a high return on the investment.

Risk

The stock market is a lot like gambling: the more you risk, the greater your chances are of receiving a greater return. It is important that you are smart about the risks you take. Risk management is when you analyze the risk and minimize it while maximizing your return. Sadly, there is a risk for each investment in the stock market. There won't always be a great return; investors lose money daily. However, there are ways to minimize risk and make smarter investments.

When investing, risk will depend on the amount of time that the investment is for. When making short-term investments, risk is crucial. If an investor plans to buy and sell the same stock on the same day, risk will play a huge role in the trade. Expecting a great return justifies that risk. However, it can easily lead to a loss. However, long-term investing (otherwise known as the "buy and hold" strategy) has reduced risk. This is because, over time, the stock's value tends to increase as a result of natural inflation. If there is a drop in the market, it will most likely repair or "correct" itself in the future. By holding onto the stock, the investor is reducing their risk of loss.

The risk may be decreased by following the market trend. If an investor familiarizes themselves with the natural flow (upward or downward) of the market and scrupulously studies the factors affecting market changes, they may easily be able to minimize risk. This is because they will have knowledge of whether the market is more likely to go up or down.

A great way to decrease risk is by portfolio diversification. This means that the stock in an investor's portfolio is spread out among different sectors, companies, and classes. While one sector decreases, it is likely that another will remain stagnant or increase. This is a great way to stay "safe" in the investing world. By spreading out your investments into the sectors of basic materials, conglomerates, consumer goods, finance, healthcare, industrial goods, services, technology, and utilities, you are ensuring that your risk is minimized and that your investments are maximized. Even if you are only interested in short-term investing or finding "hot" stocks, it is still very wise to choose a variety when investing in stock. If you can find the best performers in each sector, you will be set!

There is also a higher risk associated with certain aspects of companies. One aspect is if there are companies that aren't well-researched. This is common with companies that have very few analysts researching the stock. It is also common with new companies, as they won't have as much history and therefore will not be able to predict future earnings very well. There may also be inconsistent companies that fluctuate significantly. These are all contributors to a high-risk stock. Companies that have been increasing consistently may also be higher risks. This is because they are more volatile and may be subject to a drop in the near (or not-so-near) future. Stock that grows very quickly may show the same results.

Stocks that are extremely low-priced may also be risky. Investors might see the low price and think that it is wise to buy a great volume of that stock, hoping that it is undervalued. One is seemingly getting more for less. However, if that stock is not undervalued and may be due to an issue with the company, these stocks should be well-researched before purchasing, and the investor should be aware of the risk of these stocks.

How to Invest

There are a variety of ways that you can invest in stock. You can even have someone do it for you! The most independent way to invest is to do it yourself (or DIY). This is where you choose to manage your own portfolio and select stock for yourself. This can be cheaper, as you won't have to pay for an investment manager or full-service brokerage to manage your investments. However, this is the most independent way to invest, so you are fully responsible for your own trading activities and the selection of your stocks. This method certainly appeals to more experienced traders that have more time on their hands; however, it involves more time and research than other options. It does allow the investor to have completely personalized investments that they select themselves.

There is the option of using Robo-advisors, which typically require a small fee. Robo-advisors allow you to customize and diversify your portfolio while having it managed for you automatically. They are also quick and easily accessible. If selecting a Robo-advisor, ensure that it has a lower initial investment, minimal fees, portfolio management capabilities, and optimal investment options. Robo-advisors allow you to share your goals and create a portfolio to fit your needs. There are several Robo-advisor apps to download, which makes portfolio management simple and quick. Some offer financial advisors on-demand, which can be incredibly helpful. There is no overall "best" Robo-advisor. The best option for the investor will vary based on the needs and goals of the investor.

Stockbrokers are the ones that trade stocks by use of the stock market exchange. These are mostly online now, as opposed to being in-person. This makes for simple and quick transactions. It is also possible to set up certain features, such as automatic transfers and dividend reinvestments. It is also much cheaper and faster. There are many online stock brokers that will allow you to transfer money from the bank to an account with them and then proceed to trade stock with that money. It is important to find a broker that fits your needs and goals. It is also important to look out for minimum deposits, trading fees, promotions, and features such as education and customer support. Some brokers will offer stock selections that others won't, so be sure to look out for that as well. There are also options to link one's bank account with the brokerage, as some banks offer those services. This can make it easier to have all the finances in one place.

There is also the option to hire an investment advisor. This can be quite costly, but leads to greater peace of mind, as the advisor is a professional and will possess knowledge and experience that a beginner will not. This may be helpful for those who build up a great portfolio that needs help managing, or for those with little time to invest in their investments. It is wise to save up money before hiring an advisor (the typical amount is around $100,000). If one only has a minimal amount in stock, the cost of hiring a broker will not be outweighed by the amount generated by hiring an advisor. It may also be helpful for those with specific goals or time periods for their investments. When hiring an investor, ensure that they care about your goals, not just theirs.

In addition to choosing the right way to manage your investments, it is crucial to choose a time period that you are aiming to invest in. The "buy and hold" strategy is a common method of long-term investing. This occurs when one buys shares of stocks and holds onto it for a long time. This strategy may prove advantageous for those who want a low-risk way to receive a steady return on their investment. Investors utilizing this strategy will enjoy earning dividends, as well as a usual increase in the market value of their stock due to inflation and company success. Those who desire a quick profit may choose the short-term, high-risk day-trading option. Investors may choose to buy and sell their stock within a short time period, such as within the day, when they predict a sudden increase in the market price of the stock. This can prove to have a higher risk, as the stock may not perform as anticipated.

Leverage

To leverage is to use borrowed funds to finance an investment. This is also called margin trading and occurs when an investor borrows capital to purchase a greater amount of stock than they have the money for. It may be possible to make a larger profit than usual or experience a greater loss than usual. It allows investors to trade a large number of shares with a small amount of money.

Typically, one must create a separate margin account. This account usually requires a minimum deposit, which serves as the margin. The investor may borrow a certain percentage of the margin and must pay fees and interest. If the value of the account drops below a certain percentage, the investor must most likely pay back all or some of the loan. There is seemingly a great risk, as investors can lose a significant amount in the short-term. Although all stocks have a great amount of risk, many say that using leverage holds no more risk than standard stocks. There may even be a decreased risk as a result of the increase in leverage. It is believed to have a high risk because of the magnification of potential profit and loss. However, the risk is decreased because a larger amount of stock is traded with less capital. Those who wish to trade using leverage may trade using the options or warrants markets. They may try futures contracts or buy on margin as well. These are highly beneficial for reducing risk and increasing potential profit.

Although trading using leverage is a highly strategic move for investors, it may not always be the easiest option for beginners. It requires further education before beginning. Although it is an efficient use of capital, it requires further knowledge of how to properly use leverage to trade.

Global Economic Market

It is important to know the factors that affect both stock market prices and dividend amounts — knowing these factors can attract investors to select a stock that will be more profitable to them.

Supply and demand play a large role in the prices of stock. When demand exceeds supply, the stock prices will increase. On the other hand, a larger supply than demand will result in a decrease in price. Lower interest rates result in higher demand and, therefore, an increase in price. Higher interest rates will decrease demand and decrease price. When a company increases its dividends, that is an indication that the price of its stock will also increase. A decreased dividend amount will indicate a lower price. Expert management can increase stock prices, as the company will be more financially secure and successful. Typically, stock prices will rise during an economic recovery and fall during economic recessions. Politics and world relations can play a role in share price as well.

Dividend prices may change based on a number of factors, as well. Companies use dividends to distribute profits back to the shareholders. Some companies don't pay dividends at all. However, a company that does pay out dividends may adjust them for several reasons. Industries that are more stable will use a more consistent dividend payment method than those industries that are more uncertain. The company's ownership structure also affects its dividends. Some wish to pay out fewer dividends so as to not decrease the value of the stock. Others prefer higher dividends to increase management control. Companies that are more well-established and have been around longer will be more likely to pay out higher dividends. Companies with many shareholders will be more likely to pay out a higher dividend. A company utilizing greater leverage will be more likely to pay out lower dividends. Government policy may also affect dividend payout. More profitable companies will be more willing and able to pay out higher dividends. A company with sound liquidity will make high dividend payments possible. Dividends tend to also keep up with inflation, yet a sudden sharp increase in inflation may result in a decrease in dividend payment, as the company must recover from the sudden increase. A company with a high amount of debt may decrease its dividend. These are all factors by which dividends may be affected.

Crash vs. Correction

Unlike a dip, which is a short-term fall from an upward trend in the market, a crash is a very sudden and sharp drop in stock prices. This occurs in a short period of time and may indicate a longer period of economic hardship. It may also return quickly to its former price. A correction is a drop by ten percent of the market from a high period.

A one-day crash may occur for a great number of reasons. However, a longer crash may be caused by several factors. A declining economy may very easily lead to a crash, as well as the anticipation of a slowing economy. It may also be caused by too many investors anticipating a great chance of profit. There may also be political reasons for a crash, such as a war or an attack.

Corrections, like crashes, have reasons for occurring. If enough companies across the board experienced a great drop in earnings, a correction might occur. Fear and greed may play a role, as fear can lead to mass selling of stock, and greed can lead to a highly increased purchase of stock. If a correction is anticipated, many will sell stock and likely trigger a correction.

It is crucial for investors to understand the basics of the stock market. They should familiarize themselves with the terms of the trade, understand the concept of risk, learn the various methods of investing, understand the concept of leverage, learn how the global economic market works, and understand economic crashes versus economic corrections. By understanding these topics, the investor is setting themselves up for success.

Chapter 2: Pros and Cons

If investing in stock were easy, everyone would invest. Stock requires some time, dedication, and education before beginning. There are several reasons why individuals choose never to start investing in stock. Despite these reasons, many enjoy their stock investments and receive quite a nice profit from their investments. There are several reasons why a stock is the best way to invest your money, and there are several reasons why some choose not to invest in stock. Financial goals will differ from person to person, which is why it's crucial to learn both the pros and cons of stock. Recognizing the pros and cons will allow investors to be further educated on the stock market. It will also help investors to recognize the ways to use their money better. There are also many types of different investments and places to put one's money. The individual may opt to put their money in a bank account, invest it in real estate, purchase bonds, or purchase other tangible assets. These are all ways to use one's money, and they all have their advantages and disadvantages. Depending on the goals of the investor, there may be a better choice for the individual.

Stock: Pros and Cons

There are several ways in which stock investments are amazing; there are also some not-so-amazing aspects of stock. It is crucial to understand these aspects to further one's knowledge about stocks.

Stock is incredible in many ways. It is a great way to sit back and take advantage of the growth occurring in the economy. Over time, most companies will experience growth. Stocks allow investors to take advantage of that growth present in the economy. Additionally, stocks allow stockholders to keep up with (and stay ahead of) inflation. While inflation averages a rate of about 3.2% per year, stock averages a return of around 10% per year, that's over triple the amount! That is, however, over the longer-term. Throughout the year, stock greatly fluctuates. Yet, stock gives its investors very high returns, especially compared to other methods of investments and assets. In addition to the growth that stock offers, stockholders may enjoy the additional income given to them by dividends. Stock is also easy to buy. Because of the rise of online stockbrokers, stocks may be bought in seconds. Investing in stock is also highly customizable. The investor may choose which companies they wish to buy stock in, the amount they wish to buy of it, and how long they would like to hold on to it for. It is quite easy to diversify one's portfolio, and the options are seemingly limitless for what one may invest in. There are also several other options for buying stock. Stock is also very simple to sell. It may be sold within seconds online, and the money may be easily transferred to another account. If one needs their money quickly transferred to another account, that may be done easily. The costs of buying and selling stock are minimal, as there are typically only small fees for online transactions. Because of the ease of buying and selling stocks, stocks are highly liquid. They may easily be bought or sold, and they may be converted to cash quickly if the investor wishes to do so. Stock is also an easy way to take an ownership stake in companies. This may be only a very small portion of the company owned, yet it is quite simple to develop this relationship with the company as an owner. It may easily be stopped by selling the stocks, transferring that ownership to someone else.

Although the stock is a great way to invest one's money, there are a few disadvantages to stock investments. These must be addressed to understand the potential negative aspects of stock. However, stock investors understand these aspects, yet know that the advantages outweigh the disadvantages. Some disadvantages may also be avoided or minimized with further education. Stock is always a risk. Investors may easily lose their investment if the company does poorly enough. There may also be taxes to pay, which can further losses. If a company goes bankrupt, stockholders will be paid last. Stock is a time-consuming investment. It requires education, research, and management. Emotions may also get in the way of investments. A long-term professional trader knows not to get too caught up in the rises and falls of a stock, as it will even out over time. Day traders much dedicate their time to observing, measuring, and predicting these fluctuations, though. Stockholders tend to sell low due to fear and buy high due to greed. This is where emotions may prove detrimental to one's performance. There is also the "competition" between beginning investors and professionals. Without the proper knowledge and tools to invest, individuals will miss out on opportunities that they may have had access to otherwise. Stockholders are also competing with each other. A response to a prediction of a rise or fall can trigger a sharp rise or fall of stock, leading to the volatility of a stock. Stocks also require diversification, which may be a disadvantage if one wishes to only invest in one company or sector. If so, one risks losing all of their money in the case of economic misfortune. Those who pick the wrong stock may also suffer, as they will lose their investment in the case of poor performance.

Stocks vs. Bank Accounts

Much like stock, putting one's money into a bank account has its advantages and disadvantages. Much like stock, a bank account is a great place to hold money in and may easily be transferred to cash. The goals of both differ, however. Bank accounts serve the primary purpose of saving, while the stock market is more of an investing method. The best choice for the individual will depend on that individual's goals and financial situation. If the individual is already in debt, investing may not be the best idea. They may lose even more money than they have already lost. For those wishing to increase the amount of money that they have (and those who have the money to be able to invest), investing is wise and will yield a greater return. It is wise to diversify where one puts their money. Everyone should have some sort of emergency savings in case of job loss, medical issues, or another emergency. The typical amount to save is three months' worth of living expenses. It is also wise for those who are young to save for a house, school, and more. Those of all ages should begin saving for retirement as quickly as possible. There are always new items and services to buy, so one shouldn't wait until they want something to begin to save. A portion of each paycheck should go towards savings just in case. This will lead to a safe place for money to rest until it is spent. However, a portion of every paycheck should also go towards stocks. While one shouldn't spend all of their free money investing (just to be safe), it is wise to set aside money regularly towards investing. It is wise to take advantage of the greater return that stock provides, as opposed to leaving all of one's money in a savings account. Whereas bank accounts are generally stagnant, stocks will increase in value over time and provide many stockholders with dividends. This leads to a much greater return, as stockholders receive a 10% return on average. The typical bank account provides the user with under 1% interest. However, one must consider risk. While most bank accounts are risk-free, stock investments always come with a risk. One may select a stock that has been less risky historically, yet there may always be a slight risk. This risk is generally offset by the gains resulting from investing, though. Additionally, both investing and saving are quite easy. Because of financial operations transitioning to an online setup, transactions are quick and easy. It may take time to learn how both are set up, yet it is quite easy once one learns the system. Both offer many variations. With stock, one may invest in a variety of companies in many ways. They may also keep that stock for whichever period of time that they choose. There are many brokers out there, and one may hire an investment advisor. The same goes for saving in a banking institution. There are many banks, types of bank accounts, and options for financial advisors. There are many options for bank accounts.

A savings account is a typical account for those wishing to save their money. They have very little interest, usually only a portion of a percent. They are risk-free and easy to maintain, although they do not provide anywhere close to the return that stock does. It is possible to have an online banking account as well as a physical bank account, and many offer the ability to perform transactions online. However, some services may need to occur in a physical location, which may not be as convenient as an online service.

Checking accounts are not primarily used for savings; these are accounts that are primarily focused on a continuous flow of money in and then back out. It is easy to deposit money and checks, withdraw, and make payments from these accounts. It is also easy to transfer money in and out of these accounts. However, checking accounts typically have no interest, unlike stock investments. They certainly don't pay out dividends! They do, however, usually come with a debit card, which can be quite efficient for transactions. Although they do usually involve fees, if one overdraws their account, that will incur fees. There may also be maintenance fees and minimum balances required.

Money market accounts are ways of earning a bit higher interest than a typical savings account. However, they typically require a minimum balance. Plus, they may require fees, and the interest rates aren't usually very high. There may also be a limited amount of withdrawals per month, which may prove beneficial for those trying to save their money. This is another way to save money, though, and there is typically no risk involved.

A CD account (certificate of deposit) is the bank account with the highest interest rate, yet there is a catch. The individual will not have access to that money for the time period in which they hold it in that CD. This is good for extra money that doesn't need to be accessed, yet that money would do much better in stock investment. Although the rates are higher than a typical bank account, they still rest at about 1-5%, which does not yield nearly as much as the typical 10% return enjoyed by stockholders. The benefit, though, is the no-risk element of such accounts.

The final main type of bank account is the broad area of retirement accounts. These include IRAs and such. These are great ways to save for retirement and enjoy the tax benefits of such accounts. These accounts may also require those that hold them to not have access to their money for a certain period of time, whereas stock may be easily sold and converted to cash.

Stock vs. Real Estate

Stock and real estate are both excellent ways to invest one's money. They both give the investor ownership over an asset that generally increases in value over time. They may both be bought and sold. They may both give returns on the investment as well. However, there are several significant factors that differentiate the two and make for reasons on why either may be a better investment, depending on the person's needs, means, and goals.

Real estate may be the better choice, depending on the investor. Much like stock depends on the stock market, real estate depends on the real estate market. With both, the strategy is to buy low and sell high. Real estate may appear to be appealing because of its tangible asset. It may be easily controlled and seen in person, and investors know exactly what they are purchasing. Much like stock, real estate tends to increase in value over time. There is also the option to rent the property out, which results in great returns for the owner. Owners may also choose to hire a property manager to make their ownership experience easy. Both stock and real estate offer options for leverage, and there are many options for financing real estate. Real estate is usually easier to gain more leverage on, however. Both real estate and stock are subject to rises and drops, yet real estate fluctuations tend to be less volatile. Both require great research. It is possible to lose money with each. It is also possible to have both short-term and long-term investments with each. Stock may be bought and held over decades, then resold later. The same may be said for real estate.

Stock may be a better investment for some investors. For those wishing to gain money quickly, the stock is an easier way. Although it requires research, day traders may buy and sell the same stock on the same day, making stock trading the more liquid of the two. This can be done quickly and easily online. However, short-term real estate investments aren't quite as easy. Although there are options for selling options contracts and flipping houses, these aren't as quick as stock. It takes months to flip a house and resell it. Real estate also has many expenses associated with it. Although the stock may have fees for maintenance or transactions, these pale in comparison to the fees associated with real estate. Properties must be managed properly. The damage will need to be repaired. Bills must be paid. Financing includes both the principal payment (the payment paying off the mortgage) and interest each month. It will also cost money to pay a real estate broker to buy or sell a property, or to have someone manage the property. Both real estate and stock require diversification, and it is much quicker to diversify one's stock portfolio. A different stock may be purchased in seconds, as opposed to the months that it takes to buy a property. It also costs much more to purchase real estate. Those wishing to invest in stock may usually purchase as much or as little as they would like. Although some accounts require a minimum balance, this is not quite as much as a down payment for a house would cost an investor. Generally, at least 10% should be paid as a down payment on a house. However, there are other fees such as the commission to a real estate broker, a good faith deposit (which is customary in most transactions), and interest on the financing amount, among others. Although real estate can generate passive income when rented out, the dividends from stocks are much easier to manage and don't come after excessive fees and maintenance costs. Stock is much easier to manage, as well. The investor may buy it and forget about it, whereas real estate requires constant management

Stock vs. Bonds

Bonds are where investors will loan their money to a financial entity or government corporation. During the period of time that the investor loans their money to that borrower, that bond will increase in value. It can be thought of as interest on that bond. Over time, the value will (in theory) keep up with inflation as well.

Typically, the interest rate will be fixed; however, there are also options for the interest rate to vary for the bond. When a bond matures, the principal amount must be fully repaid, or there will be a risk of default.

Although it is good to vary where one's money is to allow for diversification and less risk, there are distinct differences in stocks and bonds that will help investors to determine where they should primarily focus their money on. Although both fluctuate, bonds tend to fluctuate much less drastically than stocks do. However, they provide less of a return for long-term investment than stocks do. Although the stock may be more volatile and may result in no return due to a loss, bonds are a more stable option. Bonds may also suffer when interest rates increase. However, the stock also fluctuates based on several market values. Bonds, although stable, do not come with the added benefit of stocks from dividends. Their value will increase over time, just as stocks do. However, many stocks also come with the bonus of providing their investors with dividends, which can help provide an additional return to the investors. Stock will yield a higher return to its investors, especially over the long-term. However, bonds are a way to obtain a reasonable return without risk. For this reason, investors may choose to invest some of their money in both; however, the stock will most likely outperform bonds for a long-term investment.

Stock vs. Physical Objects

One other way of investing is by investing in physical objects and commodities. Popular commodities include gold, collectible items, and antiques. These are all items that tend to increase in value over time, just like stock. However, there are some distinct differences between investing in these and investing in stocks.

With physical objects, the investor does have a physical item that they can see and track. However, they must sell it at a higher price than they bought it to make a profit. To do so, they must find a buyer that is willing to pay for this product, whereas stock is quite simple and quick to sell. Both require great research and calculated predictions on what to buy. With both, the investor must predict which stock or item will yield them the largest return. Both possess a risk of loss, as items and stock may both decrease in value over time. Stock and physical objects may both easily be diversified. Volatility is a concern with both, although stock tends to even out or rise in the long-term. Physical items may be predicted to rise, but there is no demand for them in the future. With physical items, the investor must find a safe place to store the items. Otherwise, they are risking the theft of these items, which will result in a complete loss. It may also be time-consuming to find and purchase these items, unlike the purchase of stock (which is quick and easy because of the Internet). Overall, it depends on the investor's preference for which of the two is a better investment for the individual.

Investors must know the pros and cons of investing in stocks. It is important to familiarize oneself with the benefits of investing in stock as opposed to other investment methods. The investor should understand the pros and cons of stocks, bank accounts, real estate, bonds, and physical objects. These are all ways that the investor may save or invest their money, and it is important to be able to make an educated decision as to which way is the best for the individual to invest.

Chapter 3: Setting Goals

It is crucial to set investing goals. This will help the investor to recognize what they are willing to put into their investing, as well as which investing methods are the best for them. If hiring an advisor, it is important to make them aware of the goals of the investor. There are several aspects of stock investing that the investor should be aware of their goals in. The individual should decide what period that they wish to invest in. They must also decide how much time each week they wish to devote to trading. Another important aspect to consider is how much the investor is willing to invest, both initially and regularly. One must consider how much risk they are willing to undertake. There should be some sort of goal with how much growth is desired, so that the investor's progress may be monitored and adjusted if needed.

Time Period

Investors should consider how long they are willing to invest their money. Some wish to hold onto their investments for a long period of time, utilizing the "buy and hold" strategy. Others prefer to buy stock and trade that same stock within the day or a few days. Some wish to purchase stock as a way to invest in their retirement. The time period that is best for the investor will depend on the investor, their goals, and their financial situation. For those who will need the money that they have invested, a shorter-term investment plan may seem more appealing. Others may choose to set aside a bit of money each month to put towards building stock for the long-term.

For those wishing to choose a lower-risk option, long-term investment is wise. This is because short-term losses will be offset by long-term gains, as the stock market tends to stabilize itself and rise and the long-term. Some may be using the stock as an alternative to a savings account and will later need access to that money. Perhaps one wishes to buy a house in two and a half years using part of the money from their stock investments. This will give the investor up to two and a half years to continue with the investment of that money.

The amount of time that the investor is willing to keep their money in stock is known as the time horizon. For instance, the time horizon for the individual who wishes to buy a house in two and a half years would be two and a half years. Before investing, the future investor should truly consider what time period that they are able to invest. They should consider whether or not they will need the money that they plan to invest at a future date and when that date is. They should also consider what they are saving towards or what their investing goal is. This will help to determine the best time period for their investment. It should also be noted whether or not there will be further money added to the investment. If so, the investor should know when the money will be added and how much will be added.

The ideal time period will vary from investor to investor. The time period will also affect other factors of the investment, such as the amount of risk that the investor should be willing to take. It may also affect the amount of time that the investor must dedicate to trading stocks.

Time to Devote to Trading

For some, trading is their primary source of income. Others may enjoy trading stock as a side hobby. There are even individuals that buy a stock only to hold onto it and essentially forget about it. Investors may choose to spend as much or as little time as they would like on their stock investments. There are several aspects of trading that require the investor to dedicate additional time to. There is education, research, trading, and management/diversification. All of these activities must be accounted for when the trader is considering how much time they are willing to spend on stock.

Before even starting out, investors must educate themselves. It is crucial to the investor's success to educate themselves on the stock market. One must familiarize themselves with all of the options that the stock market may offer them before jumping into any investment. This will help them to recognize which type of investments and strategies may best work for them and their goals. Otherwise, the investor is risking missed opportunities when it comes to investing. They must also research which stockbroker will best fit their needs. There may be one that has fewer fees, is easier for them to navigate, and offers optimal customer service. There are a number of terms that may help the investor to understand the stock market more effectively.

Investing in stock also requires great research. The investor must first educate themselves on the economy and how it works to understand the patterns of it better. They may also be able to identify better elements of the economy that will allow them to predict the movement of the economy. This may prove significant for short-term investments. It will also help the investor to identify better times to buy the stock. Day traders must study the market for hours each day. It may also help to construct charts and graphs to understand better and display the direction of the market. For these traders, it is necessary to dedicate that much time to research. Greater research will lead to greater returns. It is best for the trader to dedicate time to a number of resources to gain a better understanding of stock and be able to study multiple resources that are also studying the economy.

The investor must also conduct the actual trading. This takes a bit of time, as the investor must choose which stock they wish to purchase and sell. They must also decide how much stock they would like to purchase. This may take a bit of time; however, trading is made quite simple and quick now that most transactions are located online.

There must also be time dedicated to managing and diversifying the stockholder's portfolio. Without diversification, the investor is risking a heavy loss in their investments. Diversification allows the investor to experience losses in some areas yet make up for those losses with gains in other areas. The investor must regularly manage their portfolio. This may require writing down each of their investments or creating charts and graphs that depict their portfolio. This may show which areas may need balancing to ensure that the portfolio is properly diversified. The investor must regularly check to ensure that they are working towards their goals by trading the proper amount.

How Much to Invest

The investor must decide how much they are willing to invest. They should only invest money that they will not need in the near future. Long-term investing is the key to growing money, not saving money. Short-term investing is typically for a quick profit, yet there is the risk of losing that money. For that reason, the investor must be careful not to risk all of their money that they will need for the future. To decide how much money the investor is willing to invest will require planning. It is quite helpful to write down how much money the individual currently has total, including savings and investments. The individual should also account for all regular expenses, including but not limited to bills, groceries, gas, and entertainment. Additionally, the individual should consider how much money they earn each month (or whichever time period desired). They should also consider any current savings goals. Based on this information, the individual may start out with their total money currently. They should decide the best use of this money and make any necessary changes. Then, the individual should take their earnings and subtract necessary spending money (creating a budget for themselves). This way, the individual "pays themselves" first and has money left over to distribute appropriately. This remaining money may be used for saving or investing, depending on the goals of the individual. Each time period, the individual should follow the plan that they set for themselves to successfully invest the proper amount of money to achieve their goals.

Additionally, the investor should decide how much stock to invest in. Perhaps their goal is buying 100 shares of Company A and 50 shares of Company B. They may develop a 10-week plan, purchasing 10 shares of Company A and 5 of Company B each week. Perhaps the investor wishes to buy 240 shares of 10 companies over the course of two years. They may buy 10 shares of each company every month for those two years. There may also be monetary goals, such as working towards owning one million dollars' worth of stock over the course of several years. Whatever the goals are of the investor, there should be a set time period, set amount of companies that they wish to invest in, and a set monetary amount or share amount that the investor wishes to invest in (it may be easier to set the number of shares, as the monetary value of the stocks will fluctuate). This will ensure that the investor sets a measurable goal for themselves. It is much easier to set an ultimate goal and split it up into smaller goals. The investor may even keep a notebook for their investments and write down their goals for each week.

Risk

The investor must also how much risk they are comfortable with taking. This will be strongly affected by the other goals that the investor sets. An investor that is more educated and dedicates more time studying the market will be more comfortable with taking more risk, as their market predictions will likely be more accurate as of the result of further education and knowledge. An investor that has more to invest will be more willing to risk more, especially if they diversify their portfolio. The investor may easily dedicate a certain percentage of their investments to high-risk stocks, a certain percentage to medium-risk stocks, and the remaining percentage to low-risk stocks. An investor will also be more willing to invest in higher-risk stocks if the money that they are investing isn't necessary (it won't be needed in the near future, and the investor can afford to lose this money if necessary). There is also a somewhat inverse relationship between risk and dividends. An investor that is primarily focused on earning dividends will not be as concerned with selecting a stock that they believe will increase drastically in the future (although that is certainly an added bonus). High-risk stock that is predicted to increase drastically in the future typically doesn't give its stockholders a high dividend; however, there are always exceptions.

Growth and risk tend to be directly related. The more an investor wishes to experience growth, the more they must (usually) be willing to risk. Penny stocks, which are very affordable stocks, are typically bought in bulk with the hope that their value will multiply over time. However, these are usually high-risk investments, as these are typically companies that are just starting out. The more well-established companies will typically experience more stability, whereas these companies tend to be highly volatile.

Those who don't wish to diversify their portfolio are increasing their risk. For those who wish to only invest in one company or sector, there is a much greater risk. If that company or sector fails, there is nothing to fall back on. However, one may decrease their risk by diversifying their portfolio. That way, losses in one area may be offset by gains in another. For investors that wish to only invest in one area, though, there will be higher risk in their investments. This is a personal preference, and it is up to the investor to decide what their course of action is.

How Much Growth Desired

Much like the investor should decide how much they wish to start off with investing, they should plan how much growth they desire. Coming up with a measurable goal will help to make this easier. The investor should set goals for either each stock or their portfolio as a whole. Perhaps the investor will sell the stock when they have reached double the original value. There may also be a certain dollar threshold the stockholder wishes to reach before they sell the stock. On the other hand, the investor may wish to simply hold onto their stock and enjoy the dividends that they receive. There may not be a desire for mass growth. However, the investor shouldn't completely neglect growth; it is still crucial.

Although not every investor is highly concerned with massive growth, it is still crucial to understand the goals of the individual as far as growth is concerned. An investor who desires high growth in a short amount of time must increase their level of risk in the investments that they make. Investors who desire high growth must also (typically) put in more time into researching their investments properly. By doing so, they will be able to better select well-performing stocks. Those who invest more will experience greater growth, monetary, than those who make the same decisions but with less money. If a stock grows by 10%, the investor who bought $50,000 of that stock will yield a much higher return than the investor who bought $7,000 of it (assuming that all other factors are the same). The percentage is the same, yet the return is higher.

There are several ways to measure growth, and each investor will have their own goals regarding growth. Some investors wish to reach a certain percentage of their original investment, and then they will be willing to sell that stock. Others wish to reach a certain monetary amount before they are willing to sell their stock. Other investors don't have a certain point in growth that they desire; they have a time period that they desire to keep their stock for (such as for retirement) and simply want to make the most that they can. Some investors value growth over risk; others wish to keep their risk low, sacrificing the opportunity for additional growth.

The investor should regularly document how much their stock has grown to ensure that they are achieving their goals. If they are below their desired growth rate, adjustments may have to be made. The investor should, however, consider that stock is volatile. Nonetheless, it is important always to track one's progress to ensure that they are meeting and exceeding their personal goals. This will ensure the greatest success to the investor and ensure the greatest possible return on the investor's money.

Portfolio Diversification

The investor should decide how diverse that they would like their portfolio to be. Perhaps the investor only wishes to invest in one or two stocks and dedicate all of their investments to that area. Perhaps the investor wishes to buy a multitude of stocks in a variety of sectors. This is up to personal preference, although it may be influenced by and serve as an influence of other factors. If the right stock is selected, concentrating all of one's investments into one stock may be the right choice for the highest yield. To minimize risk, diversification is crucial. Those who desire a more long-term investment may opt for higher diversification, as the performance of different sectors may vary over the long-term. Investors who are able and willing to dedicate more time to investing will be more able to properly diversify their stock investments, as they will be able to properly research and gain knowledge on a number of stocks, as opposed to specializing in and focusing on one. Those who don't wish to or aren't able to invest a great amount may benefit from diversification, as they won't experience as much loss in the case of a sector-specific or stock-specific loss.

It is important to set goals for how many shares of stock that the investor desires to purchase over time. The investor may also set a monetary goal for the stock. They may either set a goal for specific stocks or for a certain sector. By doing so, they are ensuring proper diversification for their needs and wants. By regularly ensuring that they are keeping up with and exceeding their goals, the investor is allowing for maximum success in their investments.

Investing vs. Saving vs. Debt

The individual should take a look at their finances and determine the best course of action for their needs and goals. The easiest way to do so is first to select goals for what the individual wants to save up for or save up to. This will give the individual direction. After that, any debt should be accounted for. This is the priority before investing unless the yield of the investment outweighs the percentage of the debt. For instance, a credit card payment with a 2% interest is a lower priority than stock that yields a 10% return. If the numbers were switched, the debt should be fully repaid before investing. Although the credit card debt must still be repaid, the focus should not be solely on that repayment; if possible, extra money may go into stock instead of all extra money going towards that repayment.

After the debt is accounted for, the current money supply of the individual should be accounted for and properly disbursed into savings and investing. This allocation will vary based on the person. After this, the person's income minus expenses (bills, entertainment, gas, etc.) should be calculated. This number will reveal the regular amount of "free" money that the individual will possess. This money should go towards savings or investing, depending on the individual's goals. There should definitely be a good amount of money in savings (about three months' worth of income), and the rest may be put into investing. However, there are exceptions to the rule. If the individual does not wish to risk investing their money and has a specific savings goal, they should work towards that as well. If the individual does not have enough money yet to invest, they should either find a way to increase their income, decrease their expenses, or better balance the money they are dispersing into savings and investing.

It is crucial for the investor to set goals for themselves. This will serve as a guide to the investor as to how much to invest, how much risk to take, how much growth to aim for, how much the portfolio must be diversified, and how to decide what to do with the investor's money.

Chapter 4: Starting Out

Stock may seem incredibly intimidating for those starting out in the investment world. It seems like a completely different world, and the hardest step for most is starting out. However, it is quite simple to get started in stock investments. First, one must set goals for themselves and determine how they would like to invest in a stock. By writing down goals and ensuring that the investor's money is being used in the best possible way, the investor is helping themselves to yield the highest return on their investment. Once the individual's goals are made clear, they must plan on how to meet those goals. After this, they may choose the best investment method for meeting these goals. Then, it must be decided on where exactly the investor will go to invest their money. This is crucial, as this will be the platform by which the investor will trade their stocks. After this, the investor must open an account with whomever they choose. Before they start trading, the investor must make an initial investment using this account. While doing so, they may have to link their bank account to their stock trading account. The investor must then begin the process of buying and selling stocks using this account. Although this seems like a lengthy process, it is quite simple.

Planning and Meeting Goals

It is crucial for the investor to familiarize themselves with their goals. It is quite helpful to write down one's goals in each area and put it somewhere that is easily accessible. It is helpful to have measurable goals to reach. This way, there may be a specific time period and amount that may be assigned to the goals. It may help to come up with monthly goals. For instance, the investor may start off with the purchase of 100 shares of stock in February. They may wish to increase that to 150 shares by March, 200 shares by April, and so on. This way, the investor may have a time period to achieve their goals. This will allow them to measure their progress easily.

To set proper goals, one must reflect upon their past. How much will the investor be able to set aside for stock realistically? If one's goals are not realistic, it may become discouraging and set the investor back from their full potential. The investor must consider any past investments they have made. They must consider what worked and what did not. It is crucial to consider income and expenses when investing, and one must also consider any savings goals that they have. This will make it more apparent what may be invested in stocks.

Without a clear guide on how to invest, the investor will lack direction. This may lead to spur-of-the-moment decisions, and the investor may regret these choices later. One may set a goal for the whole year and divide that number by twelve. This may be a goal in monetary value or the number of stock shares. There must also be a bit of room for error. There may be some periods where one will not trade, as it won't be as profitable. Perhaps the market is down, and the trader does not wish to sell any stock. Perhaps the market is up, and the trader does not wish to buy any stock. There will be events such as vacations, holidays, stressful events, or emergencies.

One must also consider how much money they have. Although it is possible to double one's money in a year, it is not very likely for a beginner to do so. One may also choose to invest one time and hold it, or they may choose to invest more into their account often. This time and amount will depend on the investor and their financial situation.

The investor must also choose a strategy. They may wish to buy and sell stocks. They may wish to buy and hold stocks. They may even consider options trading. Whichever method that the investor chooses, there will be different goals to fit those strategies.

To really help the investor out, long-term goals may be set. Although planning for the next year may help the investor, longer time periods may prove even more beneficial. Perhaps the investor wishes to acquire a million dollars' worth of stock in the next ten years. Perhaps the investor wishes to save a certain amount for retirement, which they wish to have by the next 25 years. Whatever the end goal is, the investor must make that clear so that they can begin working towards it immediately. Once a proper plan is created for meeting the investor's goals, they may move to the next step.

Choosing an Investment Method

After the investor has set goals and created a plan to meet them, it is time to decide on which investment method they wish to pursue.

For those that wish to trade on their own completely, the DIY (do-it-yourself) method is the best fit. The investor may conduct all of their tradings online, and they may make transfers from the bank either manually or automatically. This will allow for full control of one's investments. There will also be complete independence over what the investor wishes to buy and sell, how much they wish to trade, and how often they wish to trade. They will, however, need to dedicate time to researching, making any transfers, trading, and other procedures. There is also a higher risk for this choice, as a beginning investor will not have the education that a financial advisor will. They also won't be under the control of a Robo-advisor. However, all of the profit that is made by the investor will be theirs to keep. They won't have to pay commission and fees outside of any required by the broker that they use.

Another method that may be utilized is the use of a Robo-advisor. This may be an alternative to hiring a financial advisor. It is a good choice for those who wish to have their investments managed for them, yet lacks the assets required to hire an investment advisor. This will allow the investor to have their portfolio automatically diversified, stocks automatically traded, and even have their taxes reduced. This may prove beneficial for those who aren't ready to completely start out in the investing world all on their own and may help ease the investor into proper stock investing. Some Robo-advisors allow a bit of flexibility when it comes to investing. This may be adjusted to fit the investor's needs. However, the investor won't gain as much knowledge as they would with DIY investing, as they would have many processes regulated for them. Some Robo-advisors do allow the investor to see exactly where their money is going and how it is being adjusted, so the investor may gain knowledge from that and learn how another would use their money to increase their return.

The least independent approach to investing in stock is by hiring a financial advisor. This method is for those who do not wish to touch their stock at all and to have it fully regulated for them. Hesitant beginners may benefit from this method. It is important to remember, however, that this method tends to be the costliest. It is most beneficial for those with higher assets and larger portfolios. It is also important to choose an investor that will work to meet the goals of the investor, not just the goals of themselves. This is why it is crucial for the investor to set specific goals for themselves and how they wish to invest their money. They may more easily communicate with the advisor their desires, and those may be carried out for them.

Choosing a Stockbroker

When investing for oneself, it is important that the proper stockbroker is chosen. This will depend on the individual's needs and wants. For some, their personal bank that they already operate with offers stock investments through their bank. This is a quick and simple option, as their money will already be linked through the bank, and they may be already familiar with their style. There may also be options for financial advisors in the bank that are free-of-charge. Otherwise, the investor must research their options before settling on a broker.

When choosing a stockbroker, the investor should research any fees (transaction fees, maintenance fees, etc.), minimum funds required to open an account, any commission collected by the stockbroker, and accessibility. The investor may prefer a certain type of formatting for their broker to have. There may also be free education, customer service, and other ways in which investing will be made easier for the investor. The investor must choose the option that will allow them to make the greatest return on their investments. The investor should keep in mind which services they are likely to use most frequently, and they should choose the broker that charges the least to use those services. There may be transactional fees, which are costs for buying and selling stocks. Many beginning investors tend to forget this, so it is important to take this into account.

To research which broker is best, there are many articles and videos online that provide comparisons of different brokerages. The investor may read into and watch these, or they may choose to ask around. Experienced investors will have already settled on their favorite and may even have some that they strongly dislike. It never hurts to ask those investors which platforms they use.

When finding the proper Robo-advisor, the tactic is similar. The advisor should be set up to meet the investor's needs. If the investor requires slight independence and choice of investments, they should pick a Robo-advisor that allows them to have some freedom of choice. There may also be some formats that allow for clearer visualization of their portfolio or are easier to navigate. The investor must also consider cost when it comes to choosing a Robo-advisor. Some may have hidden fees, so those must be considered when choosing an advisor.

Choosing a financial advisor is similar. The investor must choose the advisor that charges the least for what they're looking for. It is also crucial to choose an advisor that will work to meet the investor's needs and will be open about their strategies and procedures. The proper advisor will depend on the investor's goals and personal preferences. It may also help to interview an advisor and look for testimonials on that advisor.

Opening an Account

When opening an account, there are often a few steps that are required. This is typically not a lengthy process, but the investor should be aware of the potential steps associated with opening an account.

The first step when opening an online account is typically to create an account. This will consist of a username and password, as well as some personal information. This may include setting goals, determining which types of features that the investor wishes to use, and the experience level of the investor. This information will help to create the optimal experience for the investor.

There may also be an application for the account to ensure that the investor is qualified to hold the account. There may also be an agreement stating that the investor assumes all the risks of investing and understands that the money is not insured or guaranteed.

There may be a few days of processing required before the account may be opened and accessed. In the meantime, there is usually a requirement for the investor to make an initial transfer into the account to provide money to be able to trade with. This may also require the investor to link their account to a bank account. The broker may ask if the investor wishes to have a cash or margin account. A cash account will require that all of the stock that is bought is fully paid for ahead of time. A margin account will be borrowing money from the broker. This is another goal that must be determined prior to creating an account with the broker.

Initial Investment and Linking Accounts

During the application process, the investor will most likely be prompted to fund the account. This can be done in several ways. The investor may transfer the funds electronically via an EFT (Electronic funds transfer). This is transferring the money from a linked bank account and will most likely only take one business day to transfer. The investor may also choose to make a wire transfer, which is a transfer directly from the bank. This can occur in only minutes, yet there is often an additional fee required to undergo this process. The account may also be funded by the use of checks, although the requirements may vary from broker to broker. There may be several types of checks that aren't accepted by that broker. The investor may also choose to fund the account via asset transfer. This is a transfer from a 401(k) account or other investments. Finally, the investor may deposit stock certificates. Paper stock certificates may be mailed to the appropriate address to ensure that they are deposited into the account.

It is important to consider how much to invest in the account initially carefully. For those just starting out, there may not be much money to invest at first. The minimum investment amounts for the broker should be looked over beforehand. These amounts are typically between $500 and $5000. Although this may be a high investment for those just starting out, there are some brokerages that have lower or no minimum initial investments. There is no "perfect amount" to start out with. It will completely depend on the individual's goals and financial situation. It is notable, however, that there is always a risk for the stock. Although there are ways to lower that risk, the individual should never put all of their money into the stock. Emergencies happen, and it is important to have money for these. If money will be needed in the near future (at least the next year), the investor should strongly consider whether or not it is wise to invest this money.

For those that are unsure of how much to initially invest, they should start out with the minimum amount required and build from there. It should be money that isn't needed in the immediate future, though. Otherwise, the investor is risking losing money that is needed. It is important to remember that a large initial investment is not required to make money in stock. A small investment is better than none at all. Also, the investor may easily add more money later. It is much easier to add money than to go back in time and undo an investment. It is also not necessary for the investor to "go big" on one stock. In fact, this is not a good idea, especially for a beginner. It is important to diversify the initial investment to ensure minimum risk and maximum return. As long as the investor continues to reinvest and build their portfolio, they will experience returns on their investments. The return will also depend on the stocks chosen and the market as a whole. If the investor is planning on holding onto the stocks for the long-term, they will yield a return on their money (with some exceptions, of course). Although it is important to reduce risk by diversifying one's portfolio at first, there is "too much of a good thing." The investor shouldn't choose one share of each stock that they plan to invest in; however, they also shouldn't only buy one stock. Depending on the amount of money, goals, and wishes of the investor, it is typically recommended to start off with only a few stocks (how much "a few" will depend on the investor). This will allow the investor to focus on their investments and be able to research them, instead of being overwhelmed by a large variety of stocks.

For most brokerages, an account (typically a bank account) must be linked to the broker account. This should be an account that is easily accessible, and it should have the necessary funds. There are also helpful "hacks" to maximize the experience of a linked account. It may be set up so that funds are transferred automatically from this account. This can make it easier to reach financial investment goals. The investor must ensure that there will be adequate funds in this account to make these transfers. For instance, if $500 is transferred each month, the investor must ensure that there will be enough for this to occur each month. Additionally, there is the option to reinvest dividends. This may be set up online. Instead of taking the dividends and spending that money, they may be reinvested so that the investor may grow their money even more. There are many options for linking accounts, automating payments, and maximizing the investor's return.

By automatically transferring funds each month (or whichever time period is chosen), the investor is enjoying several benefits. First, they have set up an easy way for themselves to work towards meeting their financial goals. This will allow them to have an exact amount that they are working towards, split it up into time periods, and work towards that goal. It also allows for some automation. This will lead to less stress and work for the investor. The investor will enjoy some of the benefits experienced by using a Robo-advisor or financial advisor without having to pay many of the fees that they otherwise would have to. It can allow the investor to focus on research and trading instead of having to spend time transferring funds.

Buying and Selling Stocks

After the investor funds their account, it is time to start trading the stocks. It must be decided what stock, how much of the stock, and how the investor wishes to buy. Once these factors are decided, the investor must buy the stock. It is usually as simple as searching the stock symbol and selecting "buy." It is best to wait until the stock is at a low, but the investor must also begin investing as early as possible in experiencing the benefits of investing. When the stock is bought, it will typically take a bit to process and for the broker to receive these funds. After that, it will show up in the online portfolio of the investor. When it is time to sell this stock, the investor may typically visit their portfolio and click "sell" on the desired stock.

Starting out as a stock investor is quite simple. The investor must follow a few steps to become a stock trader. They must choose an investment method, select a stockbroker, open an account, a fund that account, and they will be ready to go.

Chapter 5: Investing Possibilities

There are many options for investing. Once the investor has determined the broker, and how much they would like to invest, it is time to determine what type of investment they wish to make. This is important to figure out before determining the specific stock that they wish to invest in. Different stocks serve different purposes; some may be highly beneficial for one investor to invest in while it may not be the best choice for another investor. It is important to determine the type of time period that the investor is wishing to invest in. For those interested in day trading or swing trading stocks, penny stocks and other speculative stocks may prove beneficial. On the other hand, dividend stocks may be beneficial for those utilizing the "buy and hold" method. The investor may wish to purchase stock the standard way or to use options. There is the option for forex stocks, as well. There are a variety of "funds," including trust funds, index funds, mutual funds, hedge funds, and ETFs. Investors should familiarize themselves with the differences between common and preferred stocks. There are also different types of orders that may be placed, which should also be differentiated by the investor. By familiarizing themselves with the different stock investment options, investors are helping to find the best choices for them in the investing world. It is crucial to learn about the different choices before jumping into any investments.

Trading vs. Buy and Hold

There are some traders that opt for a more long-term investment, choosing to buy the stock and hold onto it for a longer period. Others prefer a shorter-term investment, such as day trading or swing trading. Those that invest in the long-term have trades that last for months, years, and even decades. They buy it with the hope that it will increase over time. They may also hope to collect bonuses in the form of dividends. It is wisest to have a bit of both so that the investor can experience the benefits that both offer. This will also contribute to a more diversified portfolio. There are differences, however, in the requirements of both for the trader. Shorter-term trading requires more time and frequent research, while long-term investments are more of a source of passive income. Day traders typically spend at least a couple of hours each day studying the market and trading. Those who wish to invest in the long-term may research anytime, for as long as they wish. They may also wait as long as they would like to conduct any trades. These investors typically spend a couple of hours each month dedicated to trading. For day-trading stocks, there are usually minimum account balances to maintain, typically at least $25,000. This may completely vary based on the brokerage, yet the typical minimal fee for day-traders is higher than that of those wishing to invest in the long-term. Both require self-discipline. Short-term trading requires the trader to not act on their emotions and be patient with the amount of time that is required to dedicate to trading. Long-term traders must be patient with holding onto their investments for a long period of time.

There are two types of "shorter-term" investors: day traders and swing traders. Day traders conduct several trades a day based on analyses of the market. It takes great skill for a day trader to yield a high return on their investments. Swing traders, on the other hand, trade over the period of a few days, perhaps even a few weeks. It is a middle option between day trading and long-term investing. It takes less of a time commitment than day trading. Swing traders may experience both larger losses and gains than day traders due to the extended time period of the trade. They both require a time commitment and skills, yet day trading is a bit more demanding of the two.

While long-term investors may be on the lookout for stocks that offer dividends as well as long-term gain, short-term investors may be more likely to invest in penny stocks. These stocks are usually those of smaller companies and trade for under five dollars per share. They typically lack liquidity, as they usually trade infrequently. These are considered speculative stocks because there is a risk for the total or partial loss of the investment. Speculative stocks are stocks that the trader predicts will grow, despite a possible lack of evidence or history demonstrating such growth. Penny stocks are typically enjoyed by investors because more shares may be bought for a lower price. If there is adequate growth, this can prove highly profitable.

However, investors frequently put a large amount of money into buying penny stocks because they are "cheaper" stocks. This can prove to be a high-risk trade.

Options vs. Stocks

While stocks give you a portion of ownership in a company, options are contracts that give the owner the right to trade stocks at a particular price by a certain date. There are two types of options: puts and calls. The buyer of a call option has the right to purchase a stock at a set price before the expiration of the option. Those who buy a put option will have the right to sell a stock at a set price before the expiration of the option. The buyer or seller has the right to buy or sell options, but they are not obligated to do so. They own the asset until they sell it. When buying a call option, the investor has the right (but is not obligated) to buy the stock at a later date at a specific price. They are paying to pay for a later price. This may prove profitable if they agree to pay for a lower price, then the stock grows at that time. Call options are purchased when the investor believes that the stock price will increase in the next few months, whereas put options are purchased when the investor believes that the stock price will decrease over the next few months.

When one sells an option, they are writing that option, as options are created by individuals as opposed to companies. When one writes an option, they may be obligated to buy or sell that option before its expiration date. There are also two primary option styles: American and European. American-style options are more flexible, as they may typically be bought or sold at any time between the purchase date and date of expiration. European-style options may only be bought or sold on the expiration date. The price of an option is also known as its premium. The buyer of an option risks no more than the amount they paid for the option, as they can't lose more than the initial premium paid. The seller, on the other hand, may lose more than the original premium, as they assume the risk of having to deliver or take delivery of the stock shares.

Options are typically available only in intervals ($0.50 or $1 for typical stocks, and $2.50 or $5 for higher-priced stocks).

All options have an expiration date. Normal options may expire up to nine months from the original list date. There are also long-term equity anticipation securities (LEAPS) available, which may allow for an expiration date of up to three years. The expiration date falls on a Friday (unless there is a holiday, in which case it will be moved back one business day).

The strike price is the price that the trader predicts that the stock will be above or below by the expiration date. A contract is the number of options that the trader will buy. One contract is one hundred shares of the stock. The premium is calculated by multiplying the call price by the number of contracts bought and multiplying that number by one hundred. This is the total amount paid for all contracts.

A call option that is "in the money" has a strike price lower than the current stock price, whereas a put option that is "in the money" has a strike price that is above the current stock price. A call option that is "out of the money" has a strike price higher than the current stock price, whereas a put option that is "out of the money" has a strike price that is below the current stock price.

Forex vs. Stocks

There are a few key differences between the forex market and the stock market. They differ in their volume, liquidity, time period, commission, and focus. There are also certain skills that must be possessed to trade properly. The trader must decide which is a better fit for them.

The forex market is much bigger, as there is approximately $5 trillion traded a day. This blows away the stock market, which trades about $200 billion per day. This means that the forex market has a much larger trading volume. Traders may have their orders executed more quickly and easily, and they may trade closer to their optimal prices. This also has an effect on the market's liquidity. This higher volume leads to higher liquidity. Higher liquidity means less gaps and lower transaction costs. Because of the greater volume, there will be more liquidity at each price point. Traders may more easily enter and exit the market and get the prices that they want. Forex is over-the-counter as opposed to a traditional exchange. This allows for trading to occur virtually whenever (typically 24 hours per day, five days per week). Normal stock trading hours are from 9:30 a.m. to 4:00 p.m. The extended hours may prove beneficial for those who work another job during that time or wish to do their trading at an uncommon hour. However, that also means that the trader must possibly subject themselves to more research, as there may be trading activity at any hour of the day, even during the nighttime. Forex traders typically don't have to worry about commission, as brokers profit off of the spread (the difference between the buying and selling price). Forex has a narrower focus, as there are eight major currencies to focus on. Stock, on the other hand, has thousands of possible trades. This means that there are many more options for what to trade, yet there is also a wider range of stock to educate oneself on and choose between.

The best option for the trader will also depend on the length of time that the trader wishes to invest for. Those who look to trade in the long-term may prefer stock trading, as the forex market tends to be more volatile. They may also enjoy the steady growth and dividends that stock gives. Those who trade forex for the long-term must also have large capital to cover such volatile movements. Those who prefer to swing-trade may choose either forex or stock. They should keep in mind, however, that trading forex may require more analysis because of the volatility. Those interested in day trading may prefer forex, as it is inexpensive to trade; however, there may be a requirement for large capital account balances for certain exchanges. The "better" choice will depend on the trader and their personal preferences.

Common vs. Preferred

Both common and preferred stock are ways to hold ownership in a company. They may also both be used to attempt to profit from the future success of that company. However, there are a few key differences that separate these types of stocks.

Preferred stock does not allow its owners voting rights. Preferred stockholders also will typically receive a fixed dividend. The dividend yield will be the dollar amount of a dividend divided by the stock price, whereas common stock dividends are variable and never guaranteed. There are common stocks that don't receive any dividends. Preferred stock is also inversely related to interest rates; when interest rates rise, the value of the stock decreases, and when interest rates fall, the value of the stock increases. Common stock share values are regulated by supply and demand. Dividends are first awarded to preferred stock shareholders and then to the common stock shareholders. Preferred shareholders also possess the right to redeem shares from the market after a certain time period. The shares may be called back at a redemption rate with a premium over the purchase price. Preferred shares may also be converted to a fixed number of common shares.

Common stock is, much like its name may suggest, the most common form of stock. It allows its shareholders voting rights for board member elections and the ability to earn dividends. This stock typically outperforms preferred stocks and has a larger potential for long-term gains. This also means that losses are possible for common stock shareholders.

Order Types

There are different types of orders in stock. By having different order types, the investor has different ways that the broker may fill the trades. It can prove beneficial for the trader, as they may be able to have lower-risk options due to different order types. They may also be able to order based on their personal preferences and investing goals.

A limit order is visible to the market. The broker may buy or sell that order at a specific price or better. The stock will be bought or sold for a specific price. This order will not be filled unless the specified price is available. There is not the possibility to set the buying price higher than the current market value, as there is already a better price available. The limit order also allows for a stock to be sold once a specific price is available. The order will not be sold until the stock gets to that price. The limit order cannot be set to sell below the current market price, as a better price is already available.

A stop order is based on a price that is not yet available in the market when the order is placed. Once the price becomes available, the order will be triggered. This order is not visible to the market at first, but it will likely activate a limit order once the stop price has been met or exceeded. The investor avoids the risk of partial fills or no fills, yet the order may be filled at a worse price than the investor wished to receive. Once the stop price is met or exceeded, the order may turn into a traditional market order.

A market order is an order that is meant to execute as quickly as possible at the current (market) price. Instead of trying to get a better price in the future, the investor wishes to invest now at the price that the stock is at. While the investor may not get the best price for the stock, they do receive the benefit of a faster order. It is also more likely that the order will go through. With any order, though, there is the possibility that it will not go through. This is because orders must be available. Market orders are the most traditional order executed in the stock market. Market order prices may also fluctuate between the time that they are ordered and the time that the trade is executed.

A day order is canceled when it is not executed before the close of business on the day that the order was placed. A good-till-canceled order has no set expiration date, yet it is canceled if it is not executed by the end of a time period, which is left open when the order is placed.

Funds

There are a number of "funds" out there. There are trust funds, mutual funds, index funds, hedge funds, and ETFs. It is important that investors know the differences between these funds. This will allow for a broader knowledge of possible investment options that the investor may express an interest in.

When one buys stock shares, they are buying shares in an individual company. However, index funds serve as a bundle of stocks to track a certain index, such as the S&P 500. There may be dozens, or even thousands of stocks indirectly owned by the investor of index funds. This is also an option for those who wish to generate a good rate of return on their investments but also don't want to perform extensive, time-consuming research on individual stocks. This is a good option for a beginner, as they will not have to possess great skill in choosing the finest few stocks to invest in. It is a great way to generate passive income over the long-term, and it will also provide investors with a more diversified portfolio (that will be diversified automatically). It may not yield an abnormally high return, yet it keeps costs low, is almost fully passive, and is already more diversified than buying individual stocks.

Similar to an index fund, a mutual fund is a collection of investments as opposed to individual investments. A mutual fund is typically actively managed, unlike the passively managed index funds. Mutual funds are also typically diversified between stocks, bonds, and other securities. They may also require more fees to be paid, as they are typically actively managed by a fund manager. The fund manager will normally select the funds by hand instead of following an index.

Trust funds are legal entities that own assets. The owner must maintain trust through a legal document. The trustee decides which assets to acquire and how to distribute the money. Trust funds may be set up for beneficiaries who are too young or lack financial responsibility. A trust fund is not owned by anybody; it is a legal entity. These should not be confused with mutual funds.

A hedge fund manager will combine multiple investors' assets and trade on behalf of those investors. The investors are placing their assets in a slight pool of assets and are subject to the decisions of the hedge fund manager. On the other hand, stock transactions are handled by the investors themselves. Hedge funds will cost more due to management fees and additional fees, yet they tend to perform better due to the professional work and experience of the hedge fund manager.

Exchange-traded funds, otherwise known as ETFs, are investments in multiple securities but are traded on the market just as stocks are. Stocks do offer investors more freedom in the selection of individual stocks, yet ETFs offer investors further diversification of their portfolio. ETFs may also be index funds if they track a specific market index.

There are many investment possibilities that are open to investors. There are short-term and long-term investments, stock options, forex stocks, common and preferred stocks, different order types, and various funds to invest in. The investor should familiarize themselves with all of these possibilities and decide which fit best for them and their needs.

Chapter 6: Finding "The One"

It can be quite difficult to choose which stock or stocks that a beginning investor wishes to invest in. After all, there are thousands of options available. Investors must decide if they are wishing to invest in one stock or several stocks before deciding anything else. They must then consider what companies they already know and love and how these may be good companies to invest in (or not). The investor must also learn how to find stocks for companies that they are unfamiliar with and how to find the proper speculative stocks that will have high performances over the time period that they wish to invest for. They must also know how to invest in the time period that they are interested in. Investors must also know how to decide what sort of price of stocks they are looking for and how many shares they wish to purchase. Finally, it is crucial to learn how to analyze charts and data about stocks when researching.

One Stock or Several?

The investor must decide whether they wish to buy one stock or to buy several. Although there is a risk for all stocks, the risk may be reduced by utilizing certain strategies. While one may invest in one stock that is heavily researched, and the investor may become an "expert" on that stock, it is highly risky. If that company performs poorly, the investor will experience losses on their entire investment. If the investor chose the right stock, and it performs very well, they may experience a great return on their investment. This isn't as likely, though. Putting all of one's investment into a single stock can prove highly profitable or a great gamble. If the investor diversifies their portfolio, however, they have a smaller risk of experiencing losses on their total investment because it is spread out among several stocks.

There are several factors that may lead to a downward turn for stock. The company may have made poor decisions in its management. They may have performed badly. The economy may be weak. The industry of that stock may be in a slump. Whatever the case, it is wise to choose a variety of stocks to reduce the risk of major loss of the investment. If one stock is lacking in performance, there is bound to be another that is performing well. Although there is not a "perfect" number of stocks for one to own, it is best to own "a few" stocks. That number will vary for the investor, yet it should be a number that is high enough to allow for adequate diversification yet low enough so that the investor may easily track and manage their investments. If one has too many stocks, it can become difficult to manage all of their investments. However, too few stocks will lack the element of proper diversification.

It is wise to invest in each of the classifications of stocks. There are cyclical, countercyclical, growth, and income stocks. Cyclical stocks move with the economy. These are stocks such as airline, automotive, and real estate stocks. Countercyclical stocks tend to move in the opposite direction of the economy. These are companies that produce goods and services that are essential for life, such as utilities and pharmaceutical companies. Growth stocks tend to rise in value quite quickly, such as technology companies. Income stocks have growth that is steadier yet pay out dividends to their shareholders. Having some of each type of stock really helps to diversify one's portfolio.

Instead of buying a single stock, the investor may choose to buy multiple stocks at once in the form of a mutual fund. These may provide the investor with additional diversification and are therefore lower-risk options for buying stocks. Index funds and ETFs are also wise to invest in. Index funds will follow a certain index. ETFs will trade just as stocks do, yet they will allow for further diversification of the investor's portfolio. They will also be lower-risk investment options, as they will encompass several stocks as opposed to just one.

Investing in Familiar Companies

Beginning investors will most likely not have a solid idea of specific stocks that they wish to invest in yet. This is common for those starting out with stock investments. There are two ways that the investor may find stocks to invest in; they may research new stocks and see how others have analyzed them, or they may invest in companies that they already know and love. The investor may take into consideration what products they use every day, which stores they visit each week, or what services they use. Perhaps the investor uses a certain health care brand frequently, visits the same chain grocery store each week, or has a reliable utility company providing them with their utilities. By considering each of the goods and services that the investor uses on a daily, weekly, or monthly basis, they may determine companies that they (and many others like them) are loyal customers of. It may help to write down all of these companies and perform extensive research on them.

The investor must learn about the company's products, their performance in the market, their potential competition, and other factors about the company before investing in that particular company. Those who are familiar with the company and what it has to offer hold an advantage over those that are unaware of the company, its management, and its economic powers. One may also choose to specialize in a particular industry that they have prior knowledge of. For instance, a car enthusiast may be more aware of the automotive industry than the average consumer. For this reason, this investor will have an advantage when it comes to choosing a stock in that industry that is more likely to perform better than its competition. Although it is possible to learn about industries that one is unfamiliar with, it is wiser to stay in the sectors that one is more confident in. For instance, car enthusiasts may not have any knowledge of how the Internet works. This investor may find it wise to avoid investing in the technology industry, as much of the modern-day technology that consumers use is based around technology. Investors may walk around and get inspiration from stores nearby or even stay at home and discover who the products that they purchase are made by. These can help inspire the investor to find companies that they may research further. After this, the investor may research the company more extensively.

Perhaps the investor works for a company that has its own stocks. Those investors would have an advantage over the average investor, as they are more likely to know about the company's performance, management, and such. They may also have the option to buy stock options or use employee stock purchase plans. It may also prove highly risky if too much is invested, as the investor may lose both their job and their stock investment if the company performs poorly. There may also be emotion associated with this stock, as its performance may cause investors anxiety over their jobs.

Finding the Best New Stocks

It is important to find the right company to invest in. This will generate the highest return for the investor and build the best portfolio possible. By allowing themselves to be exposed to more unfamiliar stocks, the investor is broadening their horizons and allowing for more options of what to invest in. The investor must know what to look for when researching stocks and how to find new companies to invest in. Investors may wish to start off with a few mutual funds, and ETFs then begin to add more individual stocks to have a more diversified portfolio. They may also wish to add a certain type of stock to their portfolio. Perhaps their portfolio is mostly composed of long-term, dividend-earning stocks, and the investor wishes to add more speculative stocks to their portfolio. They may add in some high-growth stocks without dividends to their steady-growth, dividend-earning stocks. This will help to reduce risk and diversify their portfolio. They may also wish to add stocks from certain sectors to their portfolio to add additional diversification. This will also help to lower the risk of their investments, as one stock may grow while the other experiences a decline.

Those who wish to add more individual stocks may also experience a greater return than those who don't, as there may be massive growth in one stock while the others remain steady. If more stocks are owned, there is a greater likelihood that the investor will have selected a high-performing stock. By selecting stock manually, as opposed to hiring another to do so, the investor is becoming more educated and is saving themselves the money that would need to be spent on fees for fund managers or financial advisors.

To find new stocks to trade, there are a variety of ways to discover such stocks. One may acquire lists of potential stocks either online or through print. Some magazines review the best selections for stocks. These may have subscriptions, and they may have new editions each month. There are courses to take given by those who are experienced in stock training. There are videos on the Internet that speak of investors' tactics and top selections. Many articles are available to read, both online and in print. One may even search up what the best stock selections are for their investment goals. The individual may hire a fund manager or financial advisor. It is also possible to speak with those in one's life that may have more experience in investing.

The investor should look for a stock that has a fair price-to-earnings ratio (P/E). This is the company's share price divided by its net income. Although a P/E below 15 is considered cheap, it will depend on the particular company. Those with higher P/Es may be justified by rapid growth. The investor should compare this company's P/E to that of other companies in that industry to see how it compares. It is also wise to familiarize oneself with the company's revenue growth, profit margin (the difference between revenue and expenses), amount of debt, and dividend.

Investing for the Desired Time Period

Different stocks are better selections depending on the time period that the investor wishes to invest for. Those wanting to invest in the long-term may choose stocks with steady growth, dividends, and a low to medium risk. Those interested in shorter-term investments may opt for stocks that are higher-risk yet have the potential for rapid growth.

There are many ways to analyze stock to determine if it is a good investment for the long-term. The company must be financially healthy, and the stock price must be below its actual value to allow for a good deal of the purchase of the stock. The dividends must be consistent. If the company is able to pay out its dividend and increase it over time, the dividend is predictable and consistent. This means that the company is actually able to pay what it says it will, and the company is performing well enough and experiencing enough growth to raise its dividend over time. Its earnings will be optimal and will allow investors to receive a proper portion of these earnings. The investor should research the dividend earnings for at least the past five years, perhaps even the past 10 or 20 years, to truly get an idea of its earnings. The investor should also look out for stocks with lower P/Es, as that is usually an indicator of an undervalued stock. The stock should also have steadily increasing earnings over a period of years. If the price fluctuates greatly, it may not be the best long-term buy. The stock's past earnings and future earnings projections may be analyzed to make sure that the company is moving in the right direction. The valuation should also be analyzed, as a low-priced stock may fall even lower. If the company has high debt, it may not be the best buy. The investor should also evaluate the current economic condition as a whole, as the economy as a whole should be experiencing growth in the future.

Those wishing to invest in short-term stocks will have different factors to consider when analyzing the proper stocks for them. Investors may look for stocks that offer high growth or those that are highly undervalued currently. Those that experience high growth are at an average price at the moment, but they will climb to a much higher price in the near future, allowing the investor to sell their stock for a much higher price than they paid for it. These are for companies that have a high potential for growth. They tend to be valued a bit higher, though. There is a risk for these stocks, as the company may not perform as anticipated by the investor. Undervalued stocks will be lower than their competitors, although they are predicted to experience growth in the near future. These have a potential for risk, as they may not grow as anticipated. Investors may identify companies that are experiencing rapid growth and determine whether or not there is the potential for even more growth in the near future. The sales of the company should be ideal, and management should have a clear idea of how to run the company properly. The price of the stock should have an upward-trending moving average. A positive market trend is another factor to look for when buying a stock for the short-term. The investor may also look at the relative strength index (RSI), which is a comparison of that stock's strength to others like it in the market. The stochastic oscillator may also be used; this decides whether a stock is priced well based on its closing price range over time.

Prices and Shares: How Many?

The price and number of shares that an investor should be willing to pay and buy will depend on the investor's personal preferences and goals. However, there are general rules of thumb as to what the amounts of both of these should be.

The price that an investor is willing to pay will depend on the stock. $50 may be excellent for one stock, while it may be a very high price for another. This will depend on the stock's value. It may also depend on the supply and demand of that stock. The price will increase with higher demand and lower supply. On the other hand, the price will decrease if there is lower demand and higher supply. A company with higher earnings will also have an increase in the stock price. The price may also be affected based on the expectations and attitudes of investors. The price of a stock may change for a great number of reasons. Therefore, it is more important to look at the P/E than at the price itself. Similarly, an undervalued stock will be much more profitable than a simply low-priced stock. It is important for investors to know that a cheaper stock does not always equate to a better buy.

The number of shares that an investor purchases will also vary. It may depend on the price of the stock and how much money the investor has to purchase stock with. Typically, buying more shares at once is more worth the money. The typical transaction fee sits at around $7 currently. This $7 is a much higher portion of the investment when the investor purchases $100 worth of stock (7%) than when they purchase $1000 worth of stock (0.7%). However, the investor may not have the money to purchase so many shares of stock. They may also not wish to risk that many shares on one stock. Due to high commissions and stock prices, the investor may not want to buy so many shares of stock. However, they may want to make transaction fees worth it and increase their likelihood of a greater return by purchasing many shares of stock. The investor may also want to look into options, which can allow them to control many shares for only a fraction of the stock share price. This is a good alternative for some investors, yet it may not be the optimal choice for other investors.

How to Analyze Charts

To analyze a chart, the investor must know the basics. This will help to be able to understand how to read the chart and analyze it to understand more about a company and how wise of a choice it would be to invest in said company.

A stock chart will have its stock symbol, which are the few letters that identify the specific company. The chart itself will consist of the trend line, which shows the movement or trend of the stock. There may be massive growth or decline periods, which is normal for most stocks. The overall trend of the stock, however, should be that of growth. The trend line is measuring price, shown along the vertical axis, over time, shown along the horizontal axis. The charts may often be adjusted for shorter or longer periods of time. The lines of support and resistance are also important, as these are the level at which stock stays within over time. The stock will not often fall below the level of support or rise above the level of resistance. This is the typical price range of the stock, although there will certainly be extremes over time. The investor should typically buy a stock at the line of support or higher and sell at the line of resistance or lower. The chart may also show when dividends and stock splits occur. These are beneficial to watch for, as they may change the share price. The trading volumes (typically indicated by small vertical lines) determine the trend of the volumes at which the stock is traded. Increasing volumes may shift the stock price. These are the main aspects to look for when analyzing stock charts.

Selecting the first stocks may seem overwhelming at first. However, the investor may think of companies that they are already familiar with, find some that they are unfamiliar with, find stocks for the optimal time period for the individual, decide how much stock to buy, and analyze stock charts to find the best companies to invest in.

Chapter 7: Trading Strategies

When trading, there are several strategies that the investor should be aware of. They must learn the different types of trading strategies and how to utilize them. They must also differentiate between a bull and bear market, as there are different ways of handling each. The investor should learn how to properly buy low and sell high when it comes to trading. There are also strategies for what to do in a negative market trend. Additionally, there are some extra, more general strategies that beginners may use to become better traders and generate a higher return on their investment.

Trading Strategy Types

There are several different strategies that the investor may employ for trading. The investor may choose the "buy and hold" strategy, investing for the long-term. This type of investing is passive investing, as the investor typically invests and forgets, as opposed to constantly managing and changing their portfolio. They may also try active trading, which is buying and selling in the short-term. There are several strategies within this category. The investor may try day trading, swing trading, scalping, or position trading. The strategy that the investor uses will depend on their personal goals and preferences, as some strategies work better than others for different reasons.

The "buy and hold" strategy is a way of long-term investing. This is where the investor will purchase stock and leave it in their portfolio for an extended period of time, perhaps even for decades. This is a way of earning passive income, as the investor will not be required to manage this investment; they may earn money while they sleep. The stock will, typically, grow in value over time and earn the investor dividends. This is a great way to invest for those who wish to generate a steady passive income. It works for those who do not need the money immediately. It also works for investors who are not willing to put a great deal of time into investing. However, this is a long-term investment, so the investor must be willing to wait for their money and earn a steady income. They will typically not experience the immediate and rapid growth that active traders will. Those interested in long-term trading also must be willing to commit to the long-term.

Investors who wish to partake in day trading are, as the name suggests, trading within the day. They use the operating hours of the stock market to conduct their business. Unlike long-term traders, there won't be any investments taking place overnight; everything is bought and sold within the same day. This may provide traders with a higher return, as they are taking advantage of the rises and falls of the market that occur within the day.

However, this may be a higher-risk way of investing, and it requires a great deal of time to both pieces of research and engage in trading.

Position traders analyze charts of various time periods (daily, monthly, and perhaps longer) to determine the market direction trend. Instead of analyzing the short-term direction of the market, these investors will study the long-term in hopes of achieving a more accurate analysis of the market's current and future directions. They will identify trends and make predictions based on past trends.

Swing traders use the price volatility that presents itself at the end of a market trend to their advantage. These investors typically invest for more than a day but do not hold investments for the long-term. They analyze the market and determine the direction that the market will move next.

Traders that practice scalping uses the bid-ask spread gaps to their advantage. They keep these investments in the short-term. They will use the small rises and falls to their advantage and will make more but smaller movements. Instead of buying or selling a high volume of stock at once, they will trade smaller amounts more frequently.

Bear vs. Bull Markets

There are two types of markets that are commonly discussed among traders: bull markets and bear markets. These are crucial to understanding, as there are different strategies for handling each.

A bull market is what occurs when prices rise or are expected to rise. This is when there are long periods in which a large portion of security prices rise. This may occur for months or up to years. Investors, during bull markets, are more optimistic and confident that these strong results will continue for a longer period of time. This psychological effect may mask the signs of a potential decrease in the market, and investors will continue with the mindset that the market is experiencing growth. Typically, bull markets will occur when stock prices rise by twenty percent. This follows and precedes a twenty percent drop in the market. It is usually more difficult to recognize the time period in which a bull market occurs until after it has already occurred. This is because of the difficulty of predicting such a phenomenon. Bull markets occur when the economy is strong and typically occur at the same time as a strong GDP (gross domestic product) and low unemployment. This is because these events are typically associated with greater corporate profit, which will drive the stock market up. This will lead to greater investor confidence and subsequent increased demand for stocks.

For those who wish to take advantage of bull markets, there are several possibilities. It is important to buy early to take advantage of rising prices. Investors may buy and hold. They may purchase stocks in the beginning and sell them once they have grown to their peak. They may even keep buying stock as the price rises, which is called an increased buy and hold. Investors may even take advantage of retracements, which are the smaller dips within the period of growth. They may also try swing trading, which is the more active approach of taking advantage of the bull market. They may attempt to short-sell their investments during the market shifts.

A bear market, on the other hand, is where the market experiences a twenty percent drop between market highs. This is caused by an overall market decline or a major index decline. These typically last for two months or longer. It can last from several months to several years. The economy as a whole will be less strong. This is characterized by high unemployment, low disposable income, lowered productivity and decreased profits of businesses. It may also be caused by a drop-in investor confidence or a change in the tax rate or federal funds rate. Although bear markets are essentially long dips of the market, they are different from market corrections (these last less than two months).

To take advantage of a bear market, investors may short-sell their stocks. This occurs when the investor sells borrowed shares and buys them back at lower prices. For long-term investors, bear markets may be a good time to buy stocks, as they will be at much lower prices. However, this may prove to be a more high-risk strategy if the stock does not bounce back to its original value.

Buying Low and Selling High

It's commonly said that the best way to profit from stock is to "buy low, sell high." Of course, this is common sense. Investors want to get the most out of their money. The key is to try increasing the consistency of these high sells and low buys to maximize the investor's return on their investment. However, this is much easier said than done. The market is volatile, and even thorough analysis may not pan out as it's supposed to. The goal is to increase the likelihood of actually buying low and selling high. The lower the investor can buy the stock and the higher they may sell it, the better. There are a few ways to do so.

There is more than pure luck when it comes to timing the market correctly. By analyzing past trends and charting the current situation of the market, investors may more accurately predict the future movements of the stock market. However, there are constantly other factors at play. Supply, demand, unemployment, government interference, inflation, and many other factors can play a role in the outcome of the stock market. Another influential factor is investor emotion. This can cause the investor to sell out of fear and buy out of greed. At the time, these seem to be likewise decisions. However, the investor may have experienced future growth with the stocks that they sold; they may have also bought at a time where the stock was overpriced.

Those who wish to utilize market timing may be increasing their risk and profit. If the investor is able to dedicate time to researching and analyzing the market extensively, this can prove to be highly profitable. By correctly figuring out when prices will increase and decrease, investors are helping themselves increase their chances of buying low and selling high. This may be done by analyzing charts from the past few days or weeks and seeing what sort of time period that the stock is in. The investor may go further back and see how the stock has performed over the long-term. This can prove to be a more accurate way of predicting future movements of the market. However, the investor must also familiarize themselves with the company, its performance, and its management. They must additionally familiarize themselves with extensive knowledge of the global economy's performance, as this can affect individual stocks both directly and indirectly. By combining these methods of analysis and predictions, investors may be able to buy low and sell high.

It may also be possible to buy low and sell high without basing these transactions on market timing. They may buy stocks that they will hold for the long-term. These stocks should be well-developed, pay an adequate dividend, and have paid a stable dividend for at least the past decade or two. These sorts of companies should comprise at least half of the stockholder's portfolio, while the rest are "newer" companies that are still experiencing growth (such as high-performing technology companies). By doing this, the investor is "buying low." They are purchasing stocks that will increase in value over time and provide its investors with a good dividend in the meantime. The investor may sell this stock whenever they deem necessary.

Negative Market Trends

Although it would be nice for the stock market to experience growth constantly, this is not reality. There will be slight dips, corrections, crashes, bear markets, and general negative market trends. The investor must know what to do in these times.

For long-term investors, a negative market is time to buy. The investor is holding their investments for a long period of time. To them, a negative market is simply a small dip in the long-term. There will be future growth in their stocks, so why not buy when the prices are lower? General dips and such are the perfect time to buy stocks at a lower price. They must not let emotions get in the way when the market is at a low point. Many investors will sell out of fear that the decline will continue. However, the market will most often repair itself and even have great future growth. This is why it is crucial for long-term investors to hold on to their investments truly. Those who are in it for the long-term may buy at regular intervals when the market is down. At this time, they may experience losses. There may be many underpriced stocks in their portfolio. However, the prices will rise again and will turn into a great profit when the market turns around. For this reason, buying stocks at intervals during a negative market can prove to be highly profitable. They may also buy both short-term and long-term puts, which give the owner the right to sell their stocks. They may also sell their puts.

For those who are shorter-term investors, a negative market is also the time to buy. By predicting when such declines will occur, these investors may select the perfect time to buy stocks. However, they must also predict when these stocks will grow again. This takes a great analysis of both the current economic situation and how the stock has performed in the past.

Additional Beginners' Strategies

There are many different strategies that stock traders may use. Of course, there are the basic methods of trading. Investors may familiarize themselves with these. They may also build their skills over time and adjust their strategies as their goals change and as their funds increase. Some investors may choose to master one skill and gradually develop that skill through experience and education. Some investors will combine several strategies and use them. They may use different strategies for some of their portfolios. The strategy may depend on the individual stock, the length of time that they wish to invest for, the amount of risk that they desire, the performance of the market and individual stocks, and a number of other factors. Regardless, there are many strategies out there that investors may utilize. They may even create their own. There are several strategies that may prove easier for those who are just getting started with investing in a stock.

One common way to invest is to invest all of one's "extra" money. This is money that won't be needed for at least the next five years. The investor may have money in savings that they won't need to take out for a few years. This is perfect to start off with. The investor may also invest the extra money that they earn every week or month (or whatever another time period they desire) into stock. This way, the investor is not risking too much with their investments and will decrease that stress.

When starting out, the investor may want to consider keeping the majority of their portfolio low-risk, long-term stocks that offer dividends, and steady growth. Only about ten percent may be active trades. This is because the beginning investor will typically lack the knowledge and experience to be able to predict the movement of the stock market accurately. The risk of these sorts of investments will be increased, as the investor will not have experience yet in choosing the ideal stocks. Of course, there is an element of luck. An investor may, by chance, choose the right stock that will generate a high return on the investment. More often than not, however, active trades, in the beginning, will not generate great returns.

The beginning investor should come up with an extensive plan. Perhaps they will spend one-half hour a day dedicated to analyzing the market and particular stocks. Perhaps they will also dedicate three hours per week on educating themselves more on the stock market in general. They may plan to invest one thousand dollars per month into the market. By coming up with particular goals for education, investing, and analyzing, the investor is improving themselves and greatly benefitting themselves in the long-term.

It is important to become familiar with various trading strategies. Doing so will help the trader to know what to do in various situations to maximize the return on their investment. They may try buying and holding or trading. There are different strategies that may be used in a bear market versus a bull market. Buying low and selling high is always a goal of traders, and it is important to know how to do so. There are also ways to take advantage of a negative market, which can be helpful to traders. By knowing how to trade better, the investor may become more skilled in their investing.

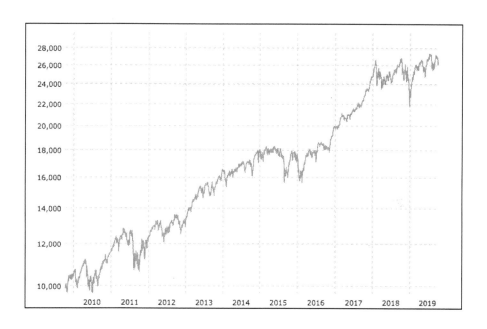

Dow Jones Index chart 2010-2019

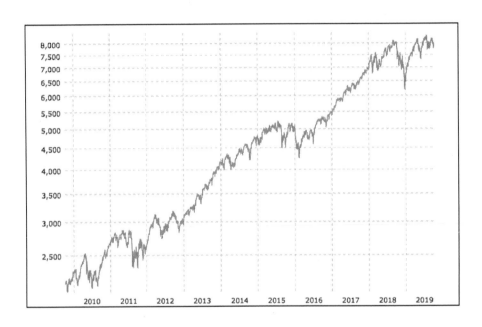

Nasdaq Index Chart 2010-2019

Chapter 8: the Big Mistakes to Avoid

In the beginning, investors will make mistakes. It is all part of the learning process. As investors become more experienced, they will learn what works and what doesn't. Although learning from one's own mistakes is an excellent way to improve, it is also beneficial to learn from others' mistakes. This is why many investors talk about the mistakes they have made; it helps to prevent others from making the same mistakes.

Diversification Issues

Beginning investors must know how to diversify their portfolios properly. Investors may make the mistake of not having enough diversification, or they have too much diversification. Perhaps they are diverse in one aspect but not in another. The investor should invest in a variety of stocks in different sectors. They should also choose stocks at different price points. They must also not have a single stock make up the majority of their portfolio. Finally, it is important to have at least a couple of long-term investments among short-term investments. There are several ways to diversify one's portfolio, and it is crucial that beginners learn the proper (and improper) methods of diversification to reach their fullest potential.

There is a great balance of diversification. There is such a thing as too much diversification and too little diversification. There is no set number for how many stocks that an investor should manage at once. This is up to the investor, their goals, and their personal preferences. The investor definitely should have more than one stock. If all of their investment is in a single stock, the performance of that one stock will determine how their entire investment performs. This can be beneficial if the stock experiences great growth. However, this can also be a high-risk move if the stock does not perform well. The investor may also have too much diversification. Especially at first, there is a lot of time that must go into research and education about the stocks that the investor owns. Although there is no "perfect" number of stocks to own, it should be enough so that there is adequate diversification, yet the investor is able to keep track of all of their investments. For instance, an individual with a full-time job will not be able to handle trading hundreds of stocks at once. This requires great research and analysis. For this reason, the investor should choose a number of stocks that they can handle to keep track of.

Investors should also have stocks of different companies in different sectors. Having just a couple of stocks or having all stocks in the same sector is also a sign of a lack of diversification. There are a few ways to help this. The investor may invest in mutual funds or index funds. This will help them to have many companies in their portfolio, and they are typically diverse already. The investor may also hand-pick companies that are in a variety of sectors to allow for proper diversification and reduce the risk of all of one's investments performing badly simultaneously.

Investors should also have a good balance of prices and amounts of stocks. It is important that the investor does not have one stock making up the majority of their portfolio. Instead, they should spread their investment among several companies quite evenly. They should also diversify the price levels of the stock that they own. While penny stocks may be cheap and have a high potential for growth, it is important to have some stocks that are of well-established companies that cost a bit more. These stocks typically are more stable (plus they may pay a dividend).

Poor Speculation

The concept of speculation is that one is investing in stock in the hopes of it growing over time. There are certain stocks that are more "speculative." These are the stocks that the investor is not certain of. They may not be well-established but hold the potential for high growth. The investor will invest in these stocks with the hope that they will generate a high return for them.

Investors must develop their skills in picking the right stocks. It is important that they don't risk it all on stocks that perform badly. For this reason, investors should familiarize themselves with how to speculate properly.

The definition of speculation seems to carry different meanings. It may mean choosing stocks that will perform well. It may also mean making predictions about the market as a whole. Economic speculations can cause actual economic events. For instance, when there is mass speculation that the stock market is going to drop, investors will begin selling out of fear. This fear gets in the way of making logical decisions, and this may cause an actual drop in the market to occur. Investors must know how to separate the fact from emotions. They must be able to sift through the rumors to discover the truth. There will constantly be speculations on the market; some may predict a massive dip while others predict great growth. Speculation can be good. If the investor puts great time and effort into their research, speculation can end up being highly profitable to them. Great returns may require the investor to take great risks. For this reason, speculation may be beneficial. It can help investors to choose the right times to buy and sell, and it can also help them to choose which stocks to buy and sell.

On the other hand, speculation can sometimes have negative effects. Investors expect companies to grow over time and provide returns that may not be realistic based on the economy and the company's revenue. Instead of reinvesting in themselves, the company is forced to meet expectations and pay its dividend out to the stockholders of the company, leading to its own destruction and an inevitable crash. This is caused by investor speculation. Instead of focusing so much on earnings per share, investors may choose to focus on creating the most cash flow as possible.

Speculation isn't all bad, though. A proper amount of speculation can regulate the health of the economy. Speculators may be able to point out when supply is running low, which will typically increase the demand and the price of stocks. This can prevent shortages from occurring. Speculators can predict a wide range of economic factors, such as growth, decline, effects of the government, supply, demand, and more. Speculators will also be able to point out the facts, yet investors must know whose advice and thoughts to listen to. The best way to learn the facts is to receive a proper education and conduct thorough research that is diversified in nature.

Improper Education and Research

It is important for investors to conduct proper research and receive proper education about the stock market. They must familiarize themselves with all of the aspects of the stock market and learn how all of those elements work together to operate. This will serve as background knowledge for the topics that they will research. Investors must research the stocks that they wish to invest in. They must also research the stocks that they already have invested in to track their performance. This is crucial for one's success in investing in stocks.

It is important to have a solid background in the stock market and to become educated on it. The investor must educate themselves enough on it to understand all of the concepts necessary for trading, but it is also important to not buy into unnecessarily expensive classes on stock education. These such courses will make promises on returns and dollar amounts of investors. What they typically don't explicitly state, however, is how much they cost and how much commission will be taken out. This is often in the fine print, and investors will learn this after it is too late. It is highly beneficial for investors to teach themselves how to invest. After all, experience is the best education. There are some topics that simply can't be taught; investors must learn for themselves how to invest in stocks. Each investor will also have individual goals for themselves, and one investor's "perfect" strategy may conflict with another's personal goals. Investing also depends on the market, which is constantly changing. An "ideal" stock to invest in one day may be a very unwise investment the next day. There is also a certain element of luck that is associated with the stock market. Although one can develop their skills in analyzing the market and predicting it more accurately, there will always be factors that are out of the control of the investor. Sudden changes may occur that the investor would not have been able to foresee.

There are, however, a few ways that one may educate themselves on the stock market. The first is by actually getting involved in the market and learning through experience. The investor may also read books on the topic (like this one). There are a number of articles available in both print and online. It is possible to learn from a mentor, friend, or even to hire a financial advisor. There are videos created by those who are already established in the market. Subscriptions are available for both e-mails and magazines. There are a number of classes, courses, seminars, and meetings for investors. It is important to diversify one's education to receive a broader knowledge of such topics. This way, the investor can learn a variety of strategies for how to invest in the stock market.

The investor must also diversify their research on stocks. They should study the company's published reports to see their net income, P/E ratio, and return on equity. Investors should look at the Form 10-K and Form 10-Q. The brokerage that the investor signed up with may also have a variety of tools for researching the market. The company's management should be researched extensively. It is important to also look at charts of the company to see how their performance has been for not only the past month or two but for the past years and even past decades. This will help to give the investor an idea of how well the company is performing currently. They can use this information to notice trends and make predictions on that company's future performance.

Inadequate Planning

Investors must plan everything out to maximize their return on their investments. Without planning, there will be no sense of direction for the investors. Investors must set goals for themselves so that they have specific achievements to work towards. It is also advisable that they plan out their schedule for trading and educating themselves to make sure that they stay on track with how much they wish to dedicate to stock. They must also figure out how much they would like to save, invest, and spend to manage their budget properly. Doing these will help investors to make the best use of their money and generate the greatest return on their investments.

Investors must set goals for themselves. Trading can become discouraging for those who fail to set specific goals for themselves. Setting goals will help the investor to stay motivated and have a path to success laid out for them. Unlike a job, stock trading does not pay by the hour. It is a self-motivated task that requires the full work of the investor. Instead of dwelling on the losses, investors may have achievements to look at and celebrate. Each trader will have their own goals that they wish to achieve, so it's important to set specific and personal goals to maximize the potential that stock has to offer. Investors should set specific goals with a specific time frame. This will challenge, motivate, and help the investor. Of course, those who attempt to generate passive income may not reap the benefits of goal setting nearly as much as active traders. Passive traders are more focused on putting their money aside and enjoying the steady growth and income that long-term investments offer. They may set goals pertaining to how much time they wish to educate themselves, how many stocks (and shares of those stocks) that they wish to acquire, and how much they wish to invest. However, active traders may get a bit more specific in their goal setting. They may be more specific about how much time they wish to dedicate to both education and analysis. They may set specific quantitative goals. There may be other goals to set, though. One goal may be not to trade when the time isn't right. Often, traders will become obsessed with the idea of trading and set quantitative goals. To meet these goals, they may make spur-of-the-moment decisions that will not benefit them in the future. It is important to learn when it may not be the best time to trade. Traders can set both quantitative and qualitative goals. There are always new strategies to utilize and various methods to try.

Investors should also have a financial plan. They should decide what percentage of their income will be used for investing. Many beginners fail to figure out the ideal amount to invest. Some start out with investing all extra money because of the newness and excitement of stock. They want to invest everything that they possibly can. However, this can prove harmful. Investors must not invest money that they will need in the near future. If losses occur and the investor needs that money, they will be out of luck. This is why it is crucial to calculate how much money must be reserved for spending, saving, and investing.

Other Common Beginners' Mistakes

There are several mistakes that beginners frequently make when first investing in a stock. It is important to learn from such mistakes to avoid making them. Although it is inevitable to make mistakes while trying something new, mistakes may be reduced by educating oneself on the potential mistakes that may be made.

In the beginning, investors may watch the market more than necessary. Although it is wise to stay updated on the market, watching it too closely will just result in anxiety about the volatility of the market and may even lead to emotional reactions to the market (buying out of greed and selling out of fear). While these may seem justified at the moment, they are typically not logical choices. Beginners may also let their ignorance drive decisions. They will put too much trust in others. While the Internet and television will be filled with helpful information, it is important to conduct individual research before buying stock. Instead of blindly following the advice of others, beginners should see for themselves what the stocks are all about. Those with long-term investments will also often forget about their goals for stock and will sell their investments out of fear. However, they may have regained all of the money that was lost and even made gains had they kept those investments for longer. Beginning traders may often neglect the aspect of risk. While traders should be willing to take some risk, it is wise to have a portfolio filled with both higher-risk and lower-risk investments just in case of an emergency. While it may seem exciting to increase the risk of investment, it may not always be wise.

It is inevitable that beginners will make mistakes in the actions that they take. These mistakes may be minimized with proper education, though. Beginners may learn how to practice proper diversification. They may learn how speculation can help (or hurt) the market. Education and research are crucial for making the best investing decisions possible. Investors should also plan how they will use their money, whether they save, spend, or invest it. By recognizing common mistakes that beginners make, beginning investors may avoid those mistakes and become better investors themselves.

Chapter 9: Mindset and Psychology

Traders must have a certain mindset when it comes to investing. Investing in stock takes a lot of self-discipline. There is a certain psychology that traders must become familiar with to be successful in their investments. There is a whole investing mindset that must be utilized to drive results. Investors must detach themselves from their emotions when investing in stock; otherwise, they risk trading out of fear and greed. Investors must also not become too attached to any stock. Although there is an art to investing, it is important that investors utilize logic to drive their actions.

Self-Discipline

Self-discipline is crucial when it comes to investing. Investors must be able to follow their plans and achieve their goals. However, many investors become tempted by the idea of better performance and abandon all logic in hopes of achieving greater returns on their investments. They will use emotions when it comes to market conditions. They may also incur greater costs because of a lack of discipline. Investors must stick with their original plan despite temptations otherwise. A short-term sacrifice will be worth it in the long-term. Although it may not be the most appealing path, the disciplined path is most often the most successful path, especially when it comes to trading.

Following the original plan and goals that the investor set is crucial. Although there are situations in which it may be more beneficial to adjust the plans due to a highly changing market or personal financial misfortune, it is better to stick to the original plan most of the time. Once the investor strays from the path originally, it will become easier to repeat that action and abandon all original plans. The investor may act without using logic and end up incurring great losses. When this happens, however, investors fail to see the consequences of their actions in the long-term. Stocks that the investors should have held onto could have resulted in gains, but the investor chose to incur losses because of a lack of discipline instead. The investor opens themselves up to allowing for loopholes whenever they deem necessary, and they hurt themselves in the long-term. The investor should create a plan for what to do if the market is negative and stick to this. They should create this plan beforehand so that they are not biased at all. However, the real discipline is actually following through with this plan when the time comes.

The investor should also be disciplined in their amount of investments. Instead of deciding last-minute use the money that they planned to set aside for stock on spending, they should stick to the original plan. It is quite easy to say that one will not invest this week and get right back to it the next week, but they have already fallen off of the plan. This can discourage the investor and lead to further lack of discipline in the future. The best way to avoid this from happening is to stick with the plan in the first place. The investor must stick with the plans for both buying and selling. They must not sell stocks that they didn't originally plan to, and they must also buy stocks that they did plan to. Regardless of market activity, the investor should still stick to their investing goals. Instead of holding back on new investments, the investor should stick to their original plan. Good habits must be formed, and the investor must not slack off despite possible obstacles. For some activities, flexibility is important. For stock, though, sticking to the plan is much more important for ensuring success. The investor must not change their portfolio based on recent market activities. This can prove to be quite difficult, especially in a bear market. However, it is usually worth it to stick through the hard times and wait for another period of growth. One's portfolio should be managed and properly rebalanced as necessary. Although it may be tempting to change this based on market conditions, the investor must hold out through the rough times. If investing for the long-term, the investor must ensure that the investments are, indeed, kept for the long-term.

Trading Psychology

The psychology that goes into trading encompasses several factors. The trader must be able to control their emotions, make quick decisions, and remain disciplined. Of course, this is in addition to being able to understand companies and predict the direction in which the stock will go. With enough practice and research, anyone can master the technical side of trading. It's those who master the psychological side that is truly successful in trading. This is what separates the good traders from the great traders. Trading psychology can be a skill crafted by practice, but it also requires the trader to shift their way of thinking.

Traders must understand the emotions that go into trading. By first understanding them, they will allow themselves to become more skillful in the way they handle such emotions. Traders must realize that fear is a natural response to bad news about the stock market. It is natural that traders will feel a sense of urgency and be tempted to liquidate their holdings, reduce risk, or otherwise sell their stocks. This, at the time, seems to be a wise move. However, traders must make decisions quickly that will benefit them in the long term, not satisfy their emotions in the short-term. By doing so, they may risk losses, but they will not miss out on the gains that they otherwise would miss out on had they given in to their emotions. It is important for traders to realize that fear stems from what people believe is a threat to them. In this instance, the threat is to their money. Traders must recognize what is making them fearful and what the best way of dealing with that fear is. It is important to come up with a plan for what to do in hypothetical scenarios before they actually occur. What is the best way to deal with a certain outcome of stock x? Traders must answer such questions before they occur so that they have a logical look at the situation. If they wait until it actually occurs, their minds will be foggy due to the emotions they feel. They may also change the way they perceive such occurrences. Instead of viewing a drop in the price of the stock as a loss, it may be viewed as a temporary dip before further growth will occur. This shift of mindset is crucial for adopting positive trading habits.

In addition to overcoming fear, investors must know how to overcome greed. If an investor holds onto a winning stock for too long, trying to get every possible amount of money they can, these gains may quickly turn to losses. Holding onto a stock for too long can prove to be less profitable than one may imagine. Yet again, traders must come up with a plan ahead of time. They must know when the right time to let go of a stock is. At the time, it seems like a wise move to the investor. They may earn more, do better than they originally thought, and make more gains. This sometimes occurs. Most of the time, however, greed is not the right choice. Traders must distinguish between greed and making wise decisions based on market changes. Sometimes, it is better to stray from the original plan. What often occurs, however, is that emotion interferes with logic, and the investor makes an unwise move by listening to their heart instead of their head.

Investors must create an extensive plan and set rules for themselves. Instead of "going with the flow," it's important to have a step-by-step plan for the investor's trading endeavors. This should be based on rational decisions, not spur-of-the-moment emotions or instincts. They must plan out when they will enter a trade and when they will exit a trade. This must be followed no matter what, and this is a great way to eliminate emotional bias. The trader may plan for certain occurrences. If unpredictable earnings occur, whether positive or negative, the trader may establish exceptions to their plan should these occur. The trader may buy a security if certain macroeconomic events occur. They may also set limits to eliminate fear and greed. These should be upper and lower limits. The upper limits will eliminate greed, and the lower will limit fear. If such a limit is reached, the trader may stop their activities for the day to eliminate emotions from taking over their activities.

Traders must also not let regret get in the way. What is in the past is in the past. It is beneficial to recognize potential mistakes, but they should not get in the way of one's performance. Perhaps the trader regrets keeping their investment for the time period that they did. Perhaps they regret the stocks that they chose. No matter what the trader could have done, it does not matter. What matters is that they use this knowledge to improve themselves in the future. This means that the next time, they may conduct more research than they did this time.

On the other hand, traders should not rationalize their mistakes. Although it is important to not dwell on the past and all of the possible ways that the trader messed up in, the trader should still recognize that they made mistakes. This is important for self-improvement, as there will always be ways in which the trader could have conducted their trades more efficiently or effectively. As a result, the trader should definitely analyze what did go wrong every time period that they wish to do so. This will make the trader better and improve their future performance and decision-making skills.

Investing Mindset

Traders may also learn different mindsets from other traders. By researching extensively and hearing how other people conduct their trades, there is much to learn. By increasing knowledge, the investor may decrease their negative emotional reactions. They will further understand the stock market and how it operates, and this will help to eliminate such reactions.

Although it is important to stick to one's plan, traders must adopt flexible mindsets. They must be willing to try new tools, buy and sell new stocks, research new companies, and trade differently. There is no "correct" way to trade. There are simply many different ways of doing so. Some may be more profitable than others. Some may work well for one trader and not well for another. Traders should be willing to slightly experiment to see what the best way for them to trade is. This may also decrease emotion when it comes to stock.

Investors should also be critical of themselves and view their trading from a logical stance. There will be certain ways to trade that will result in greater returns. Traders must be willing to reflect on their performance and see what resulted in gains and what didn't. There is always room for improvement, and traders must recognize that. Perhaps for one time period, the trader wasn't researching as thoroughly and missed certain aspects that they should have spent more time on. Perhaps the trader did let emotion influence their trades. By recognizing potential bad habits, the trader will be able to work on improving themselves and making themselves a more profitable and skillful trader for the future.

Traders must use technical analysis to drive their investing decisions. There are various ways of doing so. Perhaps the trader wishes to focus on charts. This can prove highly beneficial for seeing a visual representation of performance. The trader may have a group of investors that they seek advice from with their trades. They may have a journal to write their plan in. There are programs to use to help with investments. Whichever way the trader prefers that they conduct their business, there should be some sort of support to help logically analyze their decisions. There must be a guide.

Patience is also crucial for traders. Fear and greed, combined with a lack of patience, can truly harm the trader's ability to think quickly and make the right decision. By practicing patience, the trader will be able to decide better when the right time for buying or selling a stock is. Otherwise, the trader might be willing to jump into or out of the market despite the bad timing of doing so. Practicing patience can improve one's ability to time the market better and hold onto investments that will perform better with time while letting go of investments that have had their time.

Detaching Emotion from Stock

Emotions and trading simply don't mix. In addition to greed and fear, traders must be willing not to get attached to their stocks. Stock investments will constantly change. There will be times where it is the wisest move to invest in one stock and not another. However, traders will often become quite attached to a particular stock. The investor must be able to let go of stocks that simply aren't beneficial for them to hold on to. There is no guarantee for how well a stock will perform, as the market is constantly changing, and stocks will change, too. Investors must separate themselves from their stocks and learn when to let a particular stock go.

When trading, it is important to separate logic from emotion. Trading is a numbers game. It's all about what will benefit the trader in the long-term. While it may be easy to let fear or greed take over, to let one's mistakes hinder their future performance, or to become attached to a particular stock, these are not beneficial for one's performance. The trader must adopt a certain mindset and familiarize themselves with the proper psychology of trading. Doing so will prove highly beneficial to the trader.

Chapter 10: Additional Tips and Tricks

Mastering the basics of investing is crucial for successful trading. However, there are a few more tips and tricks that beginners may try to improve their investing experience. There are several ways for investors to maximize their investments and get the greatest return possible. Investors may also consider using a 401k, 401b, or IRA to increase their returns. Investors may try a direct stock purchase plan. They may also try a dividend reinvestment plan. Finally, there are a few additional tips and tricks that may help investors to maximize their return and improve their investing experience as a whole.

Maximizing Your Investments

There are several ways that investors may maximize their investments. Of course, practicing proper trading techniques will help investors to earn greater returns on their investments. However, there are several other ways in which investors may maximize their investments and improve the returns on those investments. They may decrease investment costs, increase diversification, rebalance, and practice other techniques to improve their investments. It is important to learn about all the possible ways to maximize one's investments because you don't know what you don't know. Every bit counts. Just saving a bit here and there will quickly add up and maximize the investments.

Investors may maximize their investments by decreasing the cost of investing. There are several ways that investing may cost one money, and that money is coming directly out of the investment. Investors may switch from hiring a financial advisor to doing the investing themselves, cutting the costs of commission. Investors commonly forget about transaction costs. There is typically a flat fee for buying stock through a broker. Instead of making many small purchases, investors may save up and only buy stocks in certain increments (for example, perhaps the investor won't buy more stocks until they have saved $1000). By doing this, a much smaller percentage of the investment is being cut out and used to cover those fees. This may require more patience, but that money will add up. Lowering one's expenses will increase their return. Instead of being spent, that money may be growing and earning a return on it. Because of compound interest, this money will earn money on itself and multiply over a period of years. This is why it's crucial to save every bit possible.

Investors must also really pay attention to their portfolios. Diversification is crucial, and it can save the investor from losing all of their investment. Markets typically fall much more quickly than markets rise. This means that the investor must prepare for such occurrences. It is important to regularly rebalance one's portfolio to ensure that it is positioned correctly for the investor to make the largest possible gains.

Investors must also truly pay attention to what they want. Maximizing one's investments will depend on the person and what their goals are. Although it is wise to listen to the advice of experts and see what other ways that one may invest, it is crucial to follow the path that is best for the goals and preferences of the individual. This is why a plan is necessary and should be followed. Investors must not stop investing. This is another way to take advantage of compound interest. The investor's portfolio should never stop growing. This growth should be due to both growths in the investment and regular contributions by the investor themselves. Despite the great returns that may be experienced in a bull market, contributions are still necessary. Bear markets should also not discourage investors from continuing to invest; this can be a great time to get a good deal on a stock!

Retirement Plans

There are several savings plans that investors can get involved with. These can help to provide the investor with additional benefits that wouldn't be available to them otherwise.

One of these plans is a 401(k). This is a retirement savings plan that will be sponsored by an employer. This will allow the individual to invest their money before taxes so that they can save and invest some of their paychecks. The investor is not required to pay taxes until they withdraw this money from their account. Investors may control how to invest their money. It is common to have mutual funds that contain stocks, bonds, and money market investments. However, there are also target-date funds, which are stocks and bonds that will decrease in risk as the investor nears their retirement age. Unlike individual investing, however, this plan may not offer its users complete freedom. For instance, most employees must work for a company for a certain period of time before gaining access to their payments. Employees may even have to work for the company for a certain period of time before being able to enroll in a 401(k) at all. There are typical costs for withdrawing from these accounts before hitting retirement age as well. There are also contribution limits for each year. Investing for oneself, however, offers more freedom, and there are no limits on investing. For those working for an employer, however, this may be a good solution to investing using the paycheck given. It is a way to utilize the ability not to be taxed on one's investments from their paycheck. Employees may also enroll in Roth 401(k)s, which are not taxed for withdrawals. The better choice will depend on both the employee and the employer, as the plans are taxed differently.

403(b) plans are similar to 401(k)s, yet there are some slight differences. Both offer matching of the investments. For instance, for every dollar the employee contributes, the employer may contribute $0.50. This can prove to be greatly helpful to investors. The major difference between these are the employees that may enroll in these plans. Those in public schools, government jobs, nonprofits, and more may register for this plan. They are not for private-sector workers. Besides this, the plans are identical in their purposes. A 403(b) plan, however, may allow for faster vesting of funds and additional contributions, although the investment options may be less plentiful.

There are also IRA plans. These are plans to save for retirement. These plans have different contribution limits, tax rules, and penalties for early withdrawals. Traditional IRAs are plans that are set up to save for retirement by the individual instead of by a company. The owner of the account will make contributions to the account. To open an account, the individual must have earned income during the year and be under 70.5 years of age. Simple IRAs are set up by small business owners for their employees. Both the owner of the account and their employee will contribute. To open an account, the employee must follow any rules set by their employer. Roth IRAs do not give a tax break when contributing, yet the retirement withdrawals are typically tax-free. Those wishing to enroll in such a plan should research their options. If given the option, the individual should research the pros and cons of their options and decide which will provide them with the best way to reach their goals. Some may not have the option given to them, yet it is wise to educate oneself on where their money is going. This may help to allow the individual to see more ways to maximize their investments.

Direct Stock Purchase Plans

Direct stock purchase plans allow investors to directly purchase stock from the company without the use of a broker. These plans may be available directly to retail investors, yet some companies will use third-party administrators to handle the transactions. They will typically have lower fees and the potential for buying shares at a discounted price. This may not be an option for all companies. These plans may also come with restrictions on when the investor may purchase shares. This plan may appeal to long-term investors that lack the money for an initial investment otherwise.

The investor may choose to sign up once for this plan, or they may sign up to make automatic and periodic investments through a transfer agent. This agent will maintain balances and record transactions. To keep costs low, transfer agents will typically carry out bulk transactions for the company each time period that they choose. Direct stock purchase plans are an alternative to using online brokerages, and they will typically cost less. Instead of paying higher transaction fees, the investor may pay a small purchase processing fee for each share that they purchase. These are usually quite a bit smaller than the transaction fees that investors must pay a brokerage. This means that the investor will have more money that they will be able to invest in. Instead of that money going to the brokerage, that money may be invested and generate a return for the investor. This can prove to be a wise move, especially for those wishing to buy a lesser amount of stocks. For those with greater funds for trading stocks, an online brokerage may prove more beneficial for the individual.

Direct stock purchase plans aren't for everyone. They will typically require investors to make a certain monthly commitment (i.e., $100) to investing. On the other hand, investors may buy stocks from a brokerage one time and never buy it again. Investors will also have to pay the market price for their stocks instead of being able to time it themselves. It may also be less convenient to create another account. However, once started, this will be an automatic investment and won't cost as much as it would purchase stocks through a broker.

This plan works by the investor making monthly deposits and those deposits being put towards purchasing shares of the company's stock. New shares (or portions of shares) will be purchased each month based on the amount of money available from deposits and dividends. This is a simple way to acquire shares of a company's stock slowly. This is also inexpensive, as these plans typically have either low costs or no costs at all. They also have low minimum deposits, usually ranging from about $100 to $500, although this may vary. This is a great plan for those who lack the financial power to invest otherwise. A common way that these purchase plans are carried out is by combining them with dividend reinvestment plans. These may be combined with the direct stock purchase plans to maximize the amount that the investor is investing in.

Dividend Reinvestment Plans

Dividend reinvestment plans allow investors to, as the name suggests, reinvest their dividends. These are typically free to sign up for and quite easy to get started in. Investors must simply check a box or click a few buttons to sign up, and the dividends that they earn will go towards reinvesting into shares of stocks. Perhaps the investor gets a dividend for stock x. If they have signed up for DRIP (Dividend Reinvestment Plan), that dividend will go towards shares (or portions of shares) of purchasing more of stock x. This is a great way to manage one's investments automatically. On the dividend payment date, the investor's dividend will go towards reinvesting in that stock.

There are ways to sign up for this through the brokerage that one trades through or through an investment company. Instead of taking out these dividends and spending them, they may be used for greater benefits to the investor. This money can help the investor to make more money. Instead of being received as a check or deposited into the investor's bank, this money may be redeposited into more stocks for the investor. The investor should keep in mind, however, that these shares will be bought at market price and will typically be bought directly from the company, which is why this is free of transaction costs. These shares will also not be marketable through stock exchanges; they must be redeemed through the company directly.

There may be some limitations to this. Although these may be commission-free for the investor and may even have discounted share prices, DRIPs may have minimum dollar amounts that must be invested. There may be a minimum purchase amount for this. This is a great way for investors to take advantage of compound interest, as they are adding the extra amount that they may not have invested otherwise. However, the dividends may still be taxable, and the shares will be illiquid. The investor, once they have signed up, will not be able to regulate how much is and is not reinvested from these dividends. It is also a great way for investors to increase the number of shares of stock that they own without paying a commission for these shares. This is a more cost-effective approach than buying stock traditionally.

Other Tips and Tricks

There are several tips and tricks that investors swear by. These may be used to the investor's advantage, or they may be ignored. The most important tip to remember when investing is to stick to one's individual goals. Despite countless advice available to investors, the best plans and actions come from the investor themselves. After all, every investor has their own personal preferences when it comes to stocks. Some wish to invest for the long-term and choose low-risk investment options while others risk more and invest for a shorter term. The investor themselves has the greatest say on what is best for them.

Some investors prefer to invest in index funds instead of investing in multiple stocks. This can decrease risk, increase diversification, and take less time to research and manage than otherwise investing in individual stocks. Investors may also consider mutual funds to lower their risk even more. These will provide investors with lower risk and higher returns. It will also help the investor to maintain a diversified portfolio. The investor may automate their investments to do so by choosing Robo-advisors or other like investment tools.

Investors must balance patience and commitment. Although it may seem wise to time the market, investors must continue to contribute during all times. There may be times, however, where the investor must practice patience to ensure that they are choosing transactions that have the best timing. The stock market is constantly changing. Above all, the investor must stick to the goals that they set prior to investing. The investor must always consider the long-term effects of their actions. While it may be tempting to respond quickly to emotional or instinctual feelings, the long-term is what must be invested. Investors must not let emotions take over their investments. It is important not to let fear control when the investor sells their stocks and not to let greed determine when to buy stocks. The investor should stick to their plan carefully. This plan should have been made prior to investing to ensure that the investor is following a logical plan that is not influenced by emotions or instincts.

Diversification is important. It is important to not only diversify the sectors and stocks that one invests in but also to diversify the amount of risk that each stock will be to the investor. This means that the investor is opening themselves up to higher returns yet still maintaining a certain level of security when it comes to investing. It is important to diversify among different classes and sectors, though. Certain industries may take a hit at once, which is why the investor should diversify their investments.

Conclusion

Thank you for making it through to the end of *Beginner's Guide to the Stock Market*; let's hope it was informative and able to provide you with all of the tools you need to achieve your goals as a stock market investor. It's difficult to make that initial leap into stock investing. For this reason, many choose never to start at all. It is crucial to becoming educated in the stock market. The individual must be aware of how the stock market and global economy work. They must familiarize themselves with various terms of the trade. There are also many different types of investments, orders, and such that the individual may make. It is crucial that the investor knows the differences between these and can decide on which methods the investor wishes to invest. However, the investor must know the pros and cons of each to reach that conclusion. The investor must educate themselves before making any further decisions on their investments and strategies for trading. There are many elements of the stock market that one must familiarize themselves with; the more that you know, the better the chance of you receiving a high return on your investment is.

The next step is to follow this book and begin your quest as a stock investor. It is important to begin by setting goals for yourself as an investor. You must consider all of the variables involved in investing. Setting goals will help provide you with a sense of direction. By using this book as a reference, you may decide on which path of investing you will choose. What will be the time period of your investment(s)? Will you purchase individual stocks or ETFs? How much risk are you willing to take in your investments? These questions, among others, must be answered to provide you with clear goals in your investing. After this, you may create an account, fund your account, and start trading. There must be research done, and you must select your stocks (which this book can help with). After this, you are on the path to success in trading.

After you have accomplished this, you must continue to conduct research on the market, monitor your stocks, and manage your portfolio. Being an investor is an ongoing process. This book can really help you to get started in learning about stock, and it may serve as a reference guide throughout your stock investing career. There will constantly be changes in the economy, the stock market will fluctuate every day, and the stocks themselves will continuously move. However, the basic concepts of stock will always be helpful to know, and this book provides its readers with those basics that are necessary for one to be successful in stock investing.

The goal of this book is to help investors, especially those who are just getting started with investing in the stock market, to learn the basic concepts of the stock market that will help them to initiate the trading process and become both successful and profitable in their investments.

If you found this book useful in any way, a review on Amazon is always appreciated!

Printed in Great Britain
by Amazon